Grant Shaw

Table of Contents

Table of Contents
Introduction 8
Chapter 1: Becoming Financially Intelligent 14
How Does Financial Intelligence Help You? 15
Self-Discipline Is the Recipe for Financial Success 18
Chapter 2: How to Adopt a Financially Intelligent Mindset 24
Changing Your Fixed Mindset Into a Growth Mindset 27
Learn to Be Disciplined Before 'Motivated' 31
Chapter 3: How to Be Disciplined and Productive With Your Money 36
Using Your Willpower as a Resource To Control Spending 37
Delaying the Instant Gratification of Spending Money 41
Is It Possible to Use up All of Your Willpower? 44
Improving Your Self-Control With Money 49
Research Study: The Effect of Willpower on a Person's Financial Decision Making 54
Chapter 4: How to Improve Self-Discipline to Save Your Money 58
Step 1: Identify What Your spending weaknesses 59
Step 2: Eliminate Your temptations 59
Step 3: Build a Financial Plan With Clear Goals 60
Step 4: Train Your Self-Discipline Every Day 61
Step 5: Build Simple and Healthy Habits 62
Step 6: Implement a Healthier Lifestyle 63
Step 7: Change Your Views on Willpower 64
Step 8: Create a Backup Plan 64
Step 9: Reward Yourself When You've Achieved 65
Step 10: Forgive Your Mistakes and Move On 65
Money-Saving Tips 65
Chapter 5: How to Build Healthy Money Habits 69
How Does a Person Form New Habits? 69
Habits That Financially Stable People Have 71
Chapter 6: Getting Rid of Your Negative Mindset With Money 90
Using Cognitive Behavioral Therapy to Challenge Your Unhealthy Thinking Patterns 92
Challenging Your Unhealthy Thinking Patterns 95
Probability Overestimation 96
Catastrophizing 97
Mind Reading 97
Personalization 98

Should Statements 98
All or Nothing Thinking 99
Selective Attention/Memory 99
Negative Core Beliefs 99
Practicing Mindfulness and Meditation....................100

Chapter 7: The Importance of Goal Setting 104
Breaking Down Your Goals Into Manageable Ones 104
Strategies to Help You Better Set and Achieve Goals..............106
Technique #1: Master New Skills Fast Using Visualization 115
Technique #2: Creating a Detailed Plan Using Visualization 117
Technique #3: Achieving Your Goals With Visualization............... 119

Chapter 8: Side Gig Ideas to Increase Your
Secondary Income 123
Remote Side Gig Ideas.. 126
Other Profitable Side Gig Ideas 131

Chapter 9: Entrepreneur Ideas to Invest and Grow
Your Money 145
Earning Potential of Side Gigs 146
Earning Potential of a Coaching/Consulting Business............149
Benefits and Drawbacks of Starting Your Own
Coaching/Consulting Business 150
Tips for Starting Your Own Coaching/Consulting Business 156
Different Types of Coaching/Consulting Ideas 161

Chapter 10: Money Management 101....................173
What Does a Good Money Manager Look Like? 173
Understanding Basic Financial Statements 176
Income Statements 177
Balance Sheets 178
Cash Flows 181
Simple Investing for Individuals...............................184
Stocks...184
Bonds 185
Commodities 187
REIT 188

Chapter 11: Basic Financial Terms for Money and
Business Management 190
Return on Investment (ROI) 190
Margins..192
Gross Profit Margin.. 193
Operating Profit Margin 194
Net Profit Margin 195
Fixed/Variable Costs 197
Variable Cost.. 197
Fixed Cost 198
Break-Even Analysis... 199

Chapter 12: Basic Must-Knows for Sales and
Expenses 203
How to Increase Sales 203
Distribution Channels 203
Sales Mix... 206

Product Selection/Differentiation 207
How to Reduce Expenses 209
Chapter 13: Basic Accounting and Financial Management Tips 213
Tips to Help You Avoid Making Bad Financial Decisions 213
Choosing the Right Accounting Method To Meet Your Needs . 216
Cash Basis Accounting 217
Accrual Basis Accounting 219
Which Accounting Method Is Best for You? 221
Chapter 14: Basic Legal Must-Knows Before Starting Your Own Business..224
Chapter 15: Prioritization Tips for Your Side Hustle228
Conclusion...232
Description 234

Introduction

Are you tired of never having any money? Do you feel like the moment you get your paycheck, that you've spent nearly all your money? Do you have large financial goals that you want to reach? If you relate to these questions, then you are someone that may need some help with money management. There isn't only one way to manage money; different people require different solutions. Some people may find that saving money is all they need to do to reach their goals, while for others, saving money may not be an option, and they may need to find ways to make more money. This book will help you in both of these topics, saving money and also creating other streams of income.

With financial security becoming a huge problem for nearly 50% of America, side hustles have become a popular option for people that are looking to get out of debt or are just interested in starting their own business. However, don't get confused with a side hustle being a full-blown standalone business – most people who start their own side hustle still have to work a traditional full-time job. The reason for this is because side hustles may not generate you any income until you get the proper traction and marketing. Having a full-time job enables you to still have the ability to pay your bills while spending some of your free time building your side-hustle, so eventually, it does start creating a separate stream of income.

So how do side hustles work? The work that needs to be completed for side hustles is usually completed during the hours outside of a person's day job. Due to this, most of the work that needs to be done usually takes place during weekends, evenings, or holidays. This way, you can still go to your 9 – 5 job and have the flexibility to do your side hustle work when you are free. There are many different types of side hustles, you can either build your own business, or you could work on a freelance, contract, or on-call for another company. Again, keep in mind that this is different than a part-time job as being employed as an 'employee' simply means that you now have two jobs. However, picking up contracts or freelance work is considered a side-hustle because you get to choose how much you work and when you do it. Later on in this book, you will be provided with more examples of different types of side hustles and small businesses – this will help you understand the difference between a part-time job and a legitimate side hustle.

If you are reading this book to get ideas on how you can start making more income, you need to decide whether you want to build an active or passive source of income or both. Let's take a look at what active and passive incomes entail. Active income means that the income you receive is for a series of services that you have performed. This includes; salaries, wages, commissions, tips, and bonuses from businesses where you have participated in. Examples of this would be someone working as a teller at the bank. They get paid in salary, and they are getting paid in exchange for the services that they are performing for one specific company. Another example would be a waiter working at a restaurant; the wages that they earn per hour is their active income, and so are the tips they make. They are actively performing services for one specific establishment and are employed by the business. Passive income is a type of income that derives from a business or enterprise where the person is not actively involved. This may include income from a rental property, a business that they have shares in, or renting out their car on share websites. In the simplest terms, active income means that you are physically doing something to obtain income, whereas passive income means you are 100% hands-off or close to it.

So now you might be wondering, why does it matter if I want active income or passive income when they both produce money for me in the end? Well, it matters because your ability to accomplish your set goals depends on you understanding these two different terms. If you are someone that wants to make enough money to live on and save for a comfortable retirement, passive income may not be enough. However, you could create a situation for yourself where you have both of these different types of income working together to speed up the process of achieving your goal. Overall, people consider side hustles to achieve financial freedom. Financial freedom means that you no longer have to work to make money actively. When a person is financially free, it usually means that they no longer have to stress or worry about money. This sounds simple, but this differs greatly in different people. Some people may define themselves as financially free if they have enough income to support their traveling, partying, and fancy vacations. To other people, financial freedom may simply mean that they don't have to worry about paying rent or their electric bill anymore.

Not only will this book guide you on generating additional sources of income, but it will also guide you on the mindset, habits, and discipline that you will require to achieve your financial goals. Creating new income streams and learning new financial skills is only 50% of the work. The other half is entirely dependent on your discipline, thoughts, and behavior related to money. Simply having financial intelligence or financial skills does not make a person a successful money manager. In reality, a person with the right mindset and habits but without ANY financial intelligence will have a higher chance of success than a person without mindset but with financial intelligence. Financial intelligence can be easily learned by reading books or going to school, but a person's discipline and mindset have to be something that is constantly practiced.

If you are reading this book with the goal of starting your own business one day, then you must also study the basic skills and mindset needed to become an entrepreneur. Entrepreneurs are different from so many other careers, as there is nobody to hold you accountable. In most jobs, you may have a manager, boss, or partner that will follow up with you on how your work is going or if you are achieving your targets and goals. With entrepreneurship, you are the sole person that is responsible for all the business duties and the managerial aspects. You are acting as the front line worker AND executive at the same time. Obviously, when you have enough success, you can hire help, but until then, you are responsible for everything starting from tedious tasks like filing all the way to business strategy. This is why learning the right mindset and habits is crucial, as without it, it is easy to become lost and distracted.

In the first half of this book, I will be covering the topics related to changing your mindset, discipline, and habits which will help you become a successful money manager. I will be teaching you about how you can improve your self-discipline to save money and how you can build good habits related to money. I will also teach you more on the topic of building the correct mindset regarding money. In the second half of this book, we will move on to more technical topics such as; side gig ideas that can create income for you, how to invest and grow your money, and low-overhead business ideas. Also, I will be teaching you about financial management, and I will be covering topics on basic finances such as how to read and write income statements, balance sheets, cash flows, ROIs, and many more.

Remember, I don't want you to get too caught up on the technical aspect of money management, as these are topics you can learn by reading and studying. Instead, I want you to keep an open mind regarding the mental aspect of saving money and achieving your goals. This part of the journey is much more difficult, and I want you to spend more of your time changing your views, improving your discipline, and building better habits. So, let's not wait any longer, and let's get started.

Chapter 1: Becoming Financially Intelligent

Financial intelligence is something that everyone has deep inside of them; however, not many people know how to use it to their full potential. Some people have more awareness of financial intelligence and are naturally better at using their money to create more money. Being financially intelligent does not mean that you have to work yourself to the bone; it simply means that you need to have a certain set of skills to help you work smartly. These skills are generally in the form of self-discipline, mindset, and good habits. The goal is to work smarter not harder!

The more you understand what financial intelligence is, the easier it will be for you to understand how to work with your money. In most cases, successful self-made people are always those with high financial intelligence. So let's first define financial intelligence. Financial intelligence is the ability to understand the ins and outs of various financial situations; this can vary from your company's finances, the finances of the company you work for, or your personal finances. In this chapter, you will learn how financial intelligence will help you and some characteristics of a financially intelligent person. In addition, I will be teaching you about how self-discipline can help you gain more financial success.

How Does Financial Intelligence Help You?

Let's take a look at how financial intelligence will help you, along with some characteristics of financially intelligent people.

1. <u>Financially intelligent people have extensive knowledge about money</u>

There is a big difference between what you know about money and what your beliefs are about money. For most people, they only understand the purchasing power than money brings, and that's about it. However, financially intelligent people know more than just that. They understand what their assets are and what their liabilities are. They understand the difference between a debit and credit card, and usually, it's the lack of knowledge that causes people to make poor financial decisions that lead them into huge debt.

2. <u>Financial intelligence can help you increase your wealth</u>

Everybody wants to increase their wealth, that is a common fact. Those with high financial intelligence are simply more natural at doing it. Regardless of whether you are an entrepreneur or not, managing your money is important. People make a lot of money out of their existing money simply because they can control their cash flow at all times. You don't have to own a business to be financially intelligent, keeping track and managing your personal expenses is enough to grow your financial intelligence and your bank account!

3. Financially intelligent people know what to do with their money

Most people think that they aren't making enough money, although this is true in some cases, many people are not utilizing their money correctly. When you aren't utilizing your money correctly, people often believe that they are not making enough. The caveat to this is that the more money a person makes, the more they are inclined to spend. Financially intelligent people are not constantly chasing after more people; they typically find success by controlling what they spend their earnings on. Typically, a financially intelligent person would aim to save at least 10% of their income that they never spend. Rather, that 10% is saved for investment purposes or kept as emergency money.

4. <u>Financially intelligent people have both short and long term goals</u>

When it comes to money goals, financially intelligent people usually have a set of short term and long term goals. The ability to differentiate between these two types of goals will keep you balanced and focused. People typically forget about their long-term goals when they are faced with the simplicity of achieving their short term goals. To build future wealth, you MUST focus on your long term goals just as much as you focus on your short term goals. Typically, short term goals would be saving up for a 2-week vacation, while long-term goals would be saving up for a mortgage or business investment. If you spend the first $2,000 you save on a vacation, none of that money will ever touch your long-term goals. Financially intelligent people make sure to always be achieving both without losing sight of either.

5. <u>Financial intelligence changes the way you relate to money</u>

As we mentioned earlier, your mindset is crucial to your entrepreneurial success. However, your mindset is also very important and has a large effect on your financial intelligence and your success at it. Successful money people control their money, and they don't let their money control them. They decide where their money goes.

Financially intelligent people are not afraid of money; they usually have complete control over all their finances.

Self-Discipline Is the Recipe for Financial Success

Mindset is crucial when it comes to financial intelligence. The way you think and feel about money has everything to do with how you spend it and save it. People with negative mindsets towards money such as; "I'm thinking of buying this new TV, even though my old one works perfectly fine" or "I worked hard for my money, I'm going to spend it and enjoy myself rather than save it." Mindsets like this cause your finances to always be in shortage and will get you stuck in a vicious cycle. Financially intelligent people typically have strong self-discipline. In many cases, self-discipline is the key to financial success.

Many researchers suggest that the single most important thing in a person's ability to become financially successful is their level of self-discipline. Self-discipline is responsible for helping people stay focused on reaching their goals, gives them the grit that they need to stick with difficult tasks, and allows them to overcome barriers and discomfort as they push to achieve greater things. Let's refresh our memory on the definition of self-discipline. Self-discipline is the ability of a person to control their impulses, reactions, behaviors, and emotions. It allows them to let go of instant gratification in exchange for long-term gain and satisfaction. It's the act of saying no when you want to say yes. Self-discipline isn't about living a restrictive and boring life without any enjoyment. In fact, it's almost impossible to be 100% self-disciplined in every single area of your life. Rather than trying to be disciplined at everything you do, you can use it to focus on the things that are most important to you. In this chapter, we will be discussing all the reasons why self-discipline is crucial to a person's financial success. We will be going through multiple reasons as to why this is true, and I will provide you with a few tips that will help increase your self-discipline overall.

1. People cannot achieve their financial goals without using self-discipline

People cannot achieve their financial goals without self-discipline, so make sure you are supplementing your goals with a self-discipline list. It will help you focus on the tasks and behaviors that you need to perform to achieve your goals. For example, one of your goals is to save $2,000 in 6 months. Your discipline list will include things like; putting aside at least $350 every month and avoid spending money on unnecessary things like fancy restaurants or video games. High self-discipline in this example would be doing everything on that list without any exception. This does not mean that you cannot reward yourself or take a break from working towards your goals, it simply means that you should get the things done on your list before you indulge in any rewards.

2. <u>Use a daily list to track your finances and to monitor unnecessary spending</u>

Make sure you are using a daily list to keep track of all the things that you need to get done to achieve your goals. Try to use online tools or just a simple notebook that can help you prioritize and organize. It feels very satisfying to be able to check off items that you've completed, and it will even motivate you to finish other tasks that are on your list just to feel the satisfaction of being able to check off another box. Make sure your to-do list works hand-in-hand with your discipline list to help yourself stay on track. A useful tip to keep in mind when you're feeling unmotivated is to start with the easiest item on the list just to get the ball rolling and build momentum. Once you complete one easy task, people will normally feel more motivated and engaged than before; this will help you get started on the rest of your list. Starting with a harder task may create apprehension about doing it; therefore, start small and work your way up.

3. <u>Figure out which obstacles are holding you back from success</u>

Different people have different things that distract them from being able to complete important tasks. For example, a person that is easily distracted by emails and people in their office might have to close their office door as soon as they get into work to get their own tasks done. They may delay any phone calls or meetings unless they're absolutely necessary to be able to complete their own set of responsibilities. This holds true for people that may be trying to lose weight. If they know that junk food is their weakness, instead of having to resist the temptation of eating junk food in their house, they can simply get rid of all the junk food in their house, so they don't have access to it. You must minimize and remove all temptations and distractions that affect you the most when it comes to reaching your most important goals.

4. <u>Share your financial goals with other people</u>

For some people, it may be easier to stick with completing a goal when they have made a public commitment to it. The thought of failing to reach a goal in front of other people can be motivation for the person to stick with it. You can also take this one step further and ask those people to hold you accountable as well. If you aren't sharing your goals with anyone, nobody will know if you have been slacking off from it. When nobody is there to hold you accountable, you will likely be less motivated to keep doing it since nobody will know if you did fail at it.

5. Use external sources or motivation as well as internal

There is a saying that goes, "don't do it for others; do it for yourself." However, some people find that they are much more disciplined when they know that their impulses, emotions, behaviors, and actions affect other people. Contrary to popular belief, it's alright to use external sources to help your motivation. Sometimes motivation coming from external sources is more powerful than internal motivation. Find the purpose that's beyond yourself that is important to you to help give you a higher chance of success.

6. Discipline is created by creating habits

When something becomes a habit, you no longer need to draw from your will power bank to get yourself to do it. For example, if your goal was to stop spending money at restaurants for lunch during the workday, get into the habit of making yourself fulfilling meals to prevent yourself from buying food when you're at the office. You will be able to see the benefits of saving money if you can stick with it. Once you see the benefit, you will have more motivation to keep doing it, and soon it becomes a habit where it will feel strange not to be making your own meals. This way, you will no longer need to draw from your bank of self-control, but instead, meal-prepping will come naturally since it has become a habit of yours.

7. <u>Stop making excuses</u>

 Don't procrastinate, or wait for tomorrow, do it now. If you fall off the wagon, that's okay. Start over immediately. Stop telling yourself that something is too hard, or there's something that you cannot change. Don't blame other people for the circumstances that you're in. Making excuses is the Kryptonite of self-discipline. Achieve a mindset that is more about "I can do this" rather than, "I'll do it tomorrow."

Chapter 2: How to Adopt a Financially Intelligent Mindset

The most important thing about becoming a successful money manager is your mindset. Your hard skills and education will never matter as much as the way you think and how you view yourself and your capabilities. To employ a financially intelligent mindset, you must improve yourself in three areas. These areas are:

- Self-discipline
- Habits
- Skills

These areas work hand in hand to ensure that you are as productive as you can be in the areas that matter the most. If you lack either one of these fundamentals, you can wave your ambitious dreams goodbye. This is the reason why not everybody can become a successful entrepreneur. Attaining these fundamentals takes a lot of work, time, and commitment. However, if you can dedicate yourself to building up these three fundamentals, you will begin to see changes in your life very quickly.

Let's talk a little about how self-discipline plays a role in helping you become a successful entrepreneur. A huge part of becoming successful, whether if it's in your career or personal life, is being able to be productive. In a world like ours today, where every day is filled to the brim with distractions, it is not easy to stay productive and not be distracted. Staying focused requires a lot of self-discipline, self-control, and willpower.

For instance, if your goal was to save $50,000 by the end of the year so you can invest it into your business, you have to properly manage your time so that you have enough energy and resources to complete tasks that will take you closer to your $50,000 goal. If you are lacking self-discipline and self-control, it will be easy for you to spend your money on attractive things like going on a vacation or buying yourself a new car. The act of self-discipline and employing that in all areas of your life is required when you are trying to achieve goals this large. In the later chapters of this book, you will be given the opportunity to learn about what self-discipline is and how you can learn and apply it to your life. Only with this, are you able to continue to develop yourself into being able to build the habits and routines that successful entrepreneurs have.

Using self-discipline, you are then developing the ability to foster other important aspects of becoming a successful entrepreneur. Mastering your self-discipline will allow you to build better habits that will ease your journey. Better habits such as improving time management, increasing persistence, and increasing organization will help you reach your goals quicker. Utilizing your newly developed self-discipline and habits, you will be able to translate that into the honing and development of new skills. People that have achieved significant success in their life have a set of skills that they are growing every single day. This will be no different for you.

Skills that successful money managers typically have included learning strong business acumen, money management, and a specialization in the industry they are in. By mastering skills in the area that you are planning to capitalize on will put you ahead of your competition. Later on in this book, I will teach you numerous ways to help you improve your existing skills and to master new ones quickly, especially in the realm of finances. One of the crucial things you have to understand before learning about developing and mastering new skills it that you must employ a growth mindset. If you are someone who has a fixed mindset – you will be faced with a tough time in terms of developing your skills. Changing your mindset from fixed to growth is a crucial step when it comes to learning and mastering new skills.

Your journey of becoming a successful money manager begins with learning self-discipline. Once you begin applying the skills of self-discipline, you can build up other fundamentals like habits, skills, and mindset. We also have to keep in mind that a journey like this isn't one without hardship. The reason why not everybody is great at money management is that some people aren't able to move past their failures or overcome obstacles. That will be addressed in this book as well.

Overall, the concept and theory behind developing yourself into a person of success are fairly simple. Self-discipline, combined with better habits, skills, and mindset with the ability to overcome failures and obstacles, is the true recipe for success. I will teach you about all of these topics, theory and actual practice included, to lead you in the right direction.

Changing Your Fixed Mindset Into a Growth Mindset

Having a growth mindset is crucial in your journey of finding success. This is especially true if you want to become a successful money manager or entrepreneur as there will be many new skills and areas you will need to learn and improve on as you grow your money. The one thing that sets most people back from reaching their goals is not knowing how to deal with failures and adversity. When it comes to achieving your goals, you have to accept that failure is a part of the process. Don't fool yourself by believing that you won't face failure along the way. Everybody does, it's a part of the process. The difference between people who find success and those who don't is simply that

27

those who did were able to learn from their failures, grow, and overcome it.

When you are faced with adversity, you must forgive yourself for any mistakes you have made and move forward. Famous snowboarder Mark McMorris, a multi-gold medal Olympian made a huge mistake that nearly cost him his life while snowboarding. Most people may have ended their athletic career right then and there in fear for their life. However, he persevered, healed, went through physiotherapy until he was well again.

This resulted in him winning more gold medals than ever before and is one of the most renowned athletes in the world. I hope that you never have to go through a life-threatening experience, but the point I'm trying to get across is that failures and mistakes are a part of the journey. Separate yourself from it and keep moving forward. Do what you can to grow and heal so you can come back stronger than before.

The 'growth mindset' is a term that was coined by Carol Dweck, who is a renowned professor at multiple universities, including Columbia University, Harvard University, and the University of Illinois. Her research with Angela Lee Duckworth stated that intelligence is not a key indicator of success. In fact, they believed that success depends on whether or not the person has a growth mindset. A fixed mindset is when a person believes that their intelligence and skills are a fixed trait. They have what they have, and that's it.

This makes the person highly concerned with what skills and intelligence they currently have, and they do not focus on what they can gain. Therefore, their activities are limited to the capacity that they think they have. However, those with growth mindsets understand that skills and intelligence is something that can be developed and learned throughout the course of their life. This can be done through education, training, or simply just even passion. They understand that their brain is a muscle that can be 'worked out' to grow stronger.

A very famous psychologist wrote a book regarding procrastination and determined that people can have one of two mindsets; either it is fixed, or they have a growth mindset. People that use a fixed mindset think that their abilities and skills cannot be changed and that they are permanent. They can only utilize their existing skills, talents, and intelligence and believe that those things cannot be further developed. Those that have a fixed mindset are under the belief that they are born with a certain set of skills. They feel they can't improve their abilities. They believe that if a person has talent, that they do not require effort to gain success. They believe that talent is something that comes naturally. A fixed mindset is a dangerous thing because it hinders a person's ability to change, learn, and grow.

Consequently, the growth mindset is one that allows a person to believe that skills, abilities, and intelligence are things that can be developed if you put in the hard work. They have the belief that a person's skills and talents are just their starting point. They believe that they are born with certain strengths, but there is no limit to what other strengths or goals they can accomplish if they put in the effort. The psychologist who studied this theory believes that people who procrastinate due to suffering from perfectionism often have a fixed mindset. What this means is that these people avoid doing the tasks that they need to do because they are afraid of the potential chance of mistakes and that completing anything that's not 100% perfect. They idealize all their work to be absolutely perfect due to the belief that if a task is not 100% matched with their current skills/talents, then they will inevitably fail; therefore, they put this task aside for another time when they feel more capable or ready.

Knowing this, you must employ a growth mindset. Every single skill you posses and the intelligence you have can be improved by putting in the effort to improve. Famous public figures of success like Oprah Winfrey, Steve Jobs, and Bill Gates all employed a growth mindset by overcoming every obstacle that got in the way.

Rather than succumbing to defeat, they worked and discovered innovative ways to overcome previous failures and found success at the end.

Think about what mindset you have right now. If you already have a growth mindset, you simply need to continue practicing it while being proactive about avoiding obstacles and overcoming failures. If you think you are someone with a fixed mindset, change it right now. Believe me when I tell you that intelligence and skills can be improved upon with time and hard work.

If you don't believe me, just try it. Pick a random skill. This could be knitting, programming, jogging, or anything that can be learned. Set goals for yourself and begin learning something new. If you can take something that you have zero skill in and become proficient in it, you have just proved to yourself that growth mindsets are real and fixed mindsets only hold you back from success.

Learn to Be Disciplined Before 'Motivated'

When people think of successful money managers or business owners, they often think that they are constantly motivated to build their business or wealth. This is not true. Motivation doesn't just appear when you ask for it; in fact, it often lacks in many people.

People that have set large goals for themselves often have the wrong mindset where they think that they need to feel fully motivated before they start working on a task/job. This mindset is unrealistic. People's motivation often does not arrive until they have started that task and are beginning to see progress. When people see progress, they start to see the fruits to their labor, and they become even more motivated to keep working until they have completed their task. You might be wondering, what about the motivation that is needed to start working altogether? The answer to this is that a person needs to have a good understanding of the 'why' and the vision of that particular job. Before you even begin working on it, you should know what the benefits are going to be. You would be surprised at how many people waste a lot of time doing work that actually does not need to be completed. Moreover, people should be using prioritization to get the most urgent and important work out of the way first. By understanding the benefits of completing a task or job, you will fully be able to estimate its importance. In terms of smaller tasks/jobs, simply understanding what the benefits are of completing that task should be enough for motivation. For larger tasks and jobs, you must have a way to measure your progress so you can further gain motivation and confidence from your work.

Here is something I want you to try in terms of utilizing self-discipline and creating your own motivation. I want you to try to break down your goal of building a successful business into the smallest steps possible. This will help you generate willpower easier as your tasks are less daunting, and it will also help you create more motivation as you begin to complete them.

Here's an example: imagine that your goal is to make an additional $50,000 of revenue in your business. It is January and of a new year, and you have no idea where to begin. Your side business is an online store that sells artisan coffee beans. Here is how I would break down this seemingly 'large' task into one that is more manageable and easier to accomplish:

1. Start with drafting a business plan for the year. If your goal is to generate $50,000 of revenue from your business, break it down into monthly and weekly revenues. $50,000 distributed over 12 months is approximately $4,200 per month. If your coffee beans sell for $40 per bag, this means you will have to approximately 104 bags of coffee per month or 26 bags of coffee per week.

2. Now that you have a monthly and weekly goal in mind, doesn't it sound less daunting? Now, take a look at your current business. How many bags of coffee are you selling per week? If you are averaging around 20 bags per week, you now know that you need to start selling at least 26 per

week to reach your $50K goal. Your next step is to start coming up with strategies to up-sell your existing clients or to market to new potential clients.

3. At this point in your business, it would be wise to expand and try to reach out to new customers. Research the best marketing strategy for coffee bean businesses and reach out to marketing agencies to get advice on this. If you feel like they are offering you a strong marketing plan, use it, and see how your results differ.

4. Analyze your results, are your sales increasing? If yes, then your marketing strategy is working. If your sales are staying the same or decreasing, then you know it is time to reevaluate your marketing strategy. Stay flexible, and don't just commit yourself to one plan. Be flexible and change your plans according to your circumstances.

5. Assess your business every single week. Are you meeting your sales by selling 26 bags per week? Are you exceeding it? By keeping track of how you're doing, you can adjust your business plan to meet your goals.

By following these steps, that one large task earning an additional $50,000 of revenue suddenly became much more manageable. Instead of thinking about that one large sum of money, you are starting with simply breaking it down to a weekly/monthly goal. From there, you can now work on your goal week by week and adjust your plan based on your experience. By taking things one step at a time, your mind becomes less overwhelmed.

Chapter 3: How to Be Disciplined and Productive With Your Money

Understanding what the psychology behind self-discipline is extremely crucial as it will help you learn what the driving factors are behind it. Successful money managers and wealthy business owners are always people that are both disciplined and productive. Learning to improve your self-discipline by understanding its nature and driving force will help you begin building more wealth.

One of the main factors that drive self-discipline is willpower. A common belief in people is that they think they can change their lives for the better if they simply could just have more willpower. If people had more willpower, everyone would be able to save responsibly for retirement, exercise regularly, stop procrastinating, avoid alcohol and drugs, and achieve all kinds of their noble goals. One survey that studied all Americans and their annual stress found that the majority of the participants reported that lacking willpower is the number one reason for not following the changes that they want for themselves.

Successful money managers who learn to improve self-discipline will find that their productivity has increased. With increased productivity, you can complete all your business-related tasks with extra time to take care of yourself. In this chapter, I will be teaching you more about self-discipline, willpower, delaying instant gratification, and self-control. I will also end this chapter with a case study about how self-discipline and willpower affect someone's financial decision making.

Using Your Willpower as a Resource To Control Spending

In the survey that we just mentioned, it was reported that the biggest obstacle when it comes to people achieving change was the lack of willpower. Even though many people often place blame upon the scarcity of their willpower for their unhealthy choices, they are still grasping on to the hope of being able to achieve it one day. Most people in this study also reported that they think willpower is something that can be taught and learned. They are absolutely correct. Some research has recently discovered many ways of how willpower can be strengthened with training and practice. On the contrary, some participants in the survey expressed that they think they would have more willpower if they had more free time to spare. However, the concept of willpower isn't something that increases automatically if a person has more time in their day. So that leads me to the next question, how can people resist when they are faced with temptation? Over the last several years, many discoveries were made about how willpower works by scientists all over the world. We will dive a little deeper into what our current understanding of willpower is.

Weak willpower isn't the only reason for a person to fail at achieving their financial goals. Psychologists in the field of willpower have built three crucial components when it comes to achieving goals. They said that you first need to set a clear goal and then establish the motivation for change. They said the second component was to monitor your behavior in regards to that goal. Willpower itself is the third and final component. If your goal is similar to the following; stop smoking, get fit, study more, or stop wasting time on the internet, willpower is an important concept to understand if you are looking to achieve any of those goals.

The bottom line of willpower is the ability to achieve long term goals by resisting temporary temptations and urges. Here are several reasons why this is beneficial. Over the course of a regular school year, psychologists performed a study that examined the self-control in a class of eighth-grade students. The researchers in this study did an initial assessment of the self-discipline within the students by getting the students, their parents, and teachers to fill out a questionnaire. They took it one step further and gave these students the task of deciding whether they want to receive $1 right away or $2 if they waited a week. At the end of the study, the results pointed to the fact that the students that had better test scores, better school attendance, better grades, and had a higher chance of being admitted to competitive high school programs all ranked high on the self-discipline assessment. These researchers found that self-discipline played a bigger role than IQ when it came to predicting academic success. Other studies have found similar evidence. In a different study, researchers asked a group of undergraduate university students to fill out self-discipline questionnaires that will be used to assess their self-control. These researchers developed a scale that helped score the students in relation to the strength of their willpower. They found that the students that had higher self-esteem, better relationship skills, higher GPA, and had less alcohol or drug abuse all had the highest self-control scores from the questionnaire.

Another study found that the benefits of willpower tend to be relevant well past university years. This self-control study was conducted in a group of 1000 people who had been tracked since birth to the age of 32. This is a long term study in New Zealand, where they wanted to learn more about the effects of self-control well into adulthood. They found that the people who had high self-control during their childhood grew up into adults that had better mental and physical health. They also had fewer substance abuse problems, criminal convictions, better financial security, and better money-saving habits. These patterns were proven even after the researchers had adjusted external influences such as socioeconomic factors, general intelligence, and these people's home lives. These findings prove why willpower is essential in almost all areas of a person's life.

Now that you have learned the importance of willpower and the role it plays in multiple stages of a person's life let's define it a little further. There are many other names used for willpower that is used interchangeably; this includes; drive, determination, self-control, resolve, and self-discipline. Some psychologists will characterize willpower in even more specific ways. Some define willpower to be:

- The capacity to overcome unwanted impulses, feelings, or thoughts.
- The ability to resist temporary urges, temptation and delay instant gratification to achieve goals that are more long-term
- The effortful and conscious regulation of oneself.
- The ability to engage a "cool" cognitive system of behavior rather than a "hot" emotional system
- A limited resource that can be depleted

Delaying the Instant Gratification of Spending Money

Delaying instant gratification is something that all money managers need to learn to do. If you cannot delay instant gratification, you will constantly find yourself spending money on things that don't positively contribute to your goals. Improving self-discipline will definitely help a lot with this. If you are unable to delay instant gratification, you may spend your money and time in all the wrong places, causing your wealth-building to be unsuccessful. Let's learn a little more about this through a famous case study.

Over 40 years ago, a famous psychologist studied self-control within children using a simple and effective test. You may have seen this study used before in modern-day experiments. His experiment is called the "marshmallow test." This test has become extremely famous over the years as it laid the groundwork and then paved the way for modern studies of self-control.

This psychologist and his colleagues began the test by showing a plate of marshmallows to a child at the preschool age. Then, the psychologist let the child know that he had to go outside for a few moments and that he would let the child make a very simple decision. If the child could wait until the psychologist came back into the room, she could have two marshmallows. If the child could not or doesn't want to wait, then she can ring the bell, which then the psychologist would come back to the room right away, but then she would only get to have one marshmallow.

Willpower can be defined as simple as the ability for a person to delay instant gratification. Children who have high self-control are able to give up the immediate gratification of eating a marshmallow so that they can be able to eat two of them at a later time. People who have quit smoking sacrifice the satisfaction of one cigarette in hopes of having better health and lower the risk of cancer in the future. Shoppers fight the urge to spend money at a mall so they can save their money for their future retirement. You probably get the point here.

This marshmallow experiment actually helped the researchers develop a framework that explains people's ability to resist or delay instant gratification. He proposed a system that he calls "hot and cool" in order to explain whether willpower will succeed or fail. The 'cool' system is naturally a cognitive one. It means that it is a thinking system that uses knowledge about feelings, sensations, goals, and actions that remind oneself, for example, why the marshmallow shouldn't be eaten. The cool system is very reflective, while the hot system is more emotional and impulsive. The hot system is responsible for quick and reflex-based responses to specific triggers, for example, eating the single marshmallow without thinking about the long term ramifications. To put this in layman's terms, if this framework were a cartoon, the hot system would be the devil, and the cool system would be the angel on your shoulder.

When somebody's willpower fails, their hot system essentially overrides their cool system, which leads them to make impulsive actions. However, some people are more or less affected by the hot system triggers. That susceptibility to emotional responses plays a big role in influencing a person's behavior throughout life. The same researcher discovered that when he revisited his experiment with the children that had now grown up into adolescents, he found that those who waited longer to have two marshmallows were more likely to have higher SAT grades. The parents were more likely to rate them of having better ability to handle stress, plan, respond to reason, and exhibit self-control in frustrating situations and could concentrate better without being easily distracted.

Funny enough, the marshmallow study didn't end there. A few other researchers tracked down almost 60 people who are now middle-aged, who had previously been a part of the marshmallow experiment as young children. These psychologists proceeded to test the participants' willpower strength using a task that's been proven to prove self-control within adults. Surprisingly, the participants' various willpower strengths had been very consistent over the last 40 years. Overall, they found that the children who were not successful in resisting the first marshmallow did poorly on the self-control tasks as an adult and that their hot stimuli seem to be consistent throughout their lifetime. They also began to study brain activity in some of the participants by using magnetic resonance technology. When these participants were presented with tempting stimuli, those who had low willpower exhibited brain patterns that were very different from the brain patterns of those that had strong willpower. They discovered that the prefrontal cortex (this is the region of the brain that controls choice-making functions) was more active in the participants who had stronger willpower and the ventral striatum (an area of the brain that is focused on processing rewards and desires) showed increased activity in the participants who had weaker willpower.

Is It Possible to Use up All of Your Willpower?

If you are someone that's looking to grow your wealth, you are likely exerting willpower and self-discipline all the time to ensure you are making the best decisions you can for your financial well-being. In this sub-chapter, you will be learning about the concept of willpower and whether or not it is possible to run out of it. Let's take a look at something called the hot-cold framework.

The hot-cold framework does a great job of explaining people's ability to delay gratification. Still, there is another theory that is called 'willpower depletion' that has emerged in recent years to explain what happens to people after they have resisted multiple temptations. Everyone exerts willpower every day in one form or another. People resist to surf the web or go on social media instead of finishing their work. They may choose a salad when they are craving a slice of pizza. They may hold their tongue rather than make a snide remark. Recent growing research indicates that resisting temptations takes a mental toll on a person. Some people describe willpower as a muscle that can get tired if overused.

The earliest discoveries of this concept came from a study that was conducted in Germany. The researcher brought participants into a room that smelled like fresh-baked cookies. The participants sat down at the table that held a bowl of radishes and a plate of those freshly baked cookies. The researchers asked some of the participants to taste those cookies while others were asked to try the radishes. After this, the participants were assigned to complete a difficult geometric puzzle in 30 minutes. The researchers found that the participants who had to eat the radishes (therefore resisting the urge to eat the cookies) took 8 minutes to give up on the puzzle while the participants who got to eat the cookies tried to complete the puzzle for 19 minutes. The evidence here seems as if the people who used their willpower to resist eating the cookies drained their resources for future situations.

In the late 90s, this research was published, and since then, numerous other studies have begun looking into willpower depletion or otherwise known as ego depletion. One study, for example, the participants were asked to hold back and suppress any feelings they had while they watched an emotional film. These participants then participated in a physical stamina test but gave up sooner than the participants who watched the movie and reacted normally without any suppression.

Depleting willpower is very common in today's society. You have probably tried to make yourself diplomatic when you are dealing with an aggravating customer or forced to fake happiness when your in-laws come to stay with you for an extended period of time. You must have realized that certain social interacts demand the use of willpower. There is also existing research that has proven that people interacting with others and maintaining relationships often is a high depleter of willpower.

Willpower depletion is not solely just a simple case of feeling tired. During another study by the same researcher, she had the participants in her study go through a whole day of sleep deprivation and then asked them to watch a movie but to suppress their emotions and reactions during it. She then proceeded to test the strength of the participant's self-control and found that those participants who didn't get sleep were not much more likely to be depleted of willpower compared to those who got a full night's sleep.

So if willpower isn't related to physical fatigue, then what exactly is it? Research studies have recently discovered a few different mechanisms that are possibly responsible for willpower depletion, some that were at the biological level. The researchers found that the people whose willpower became depleted after completing self-control tasks showed lowered activity in the region of their brain that controlled cognition. When willpower is being tested, a person's brain may begin to function differently.

Some other evidence indicates that people who have depleted willpower might be on low on fuel quite literally. Since the brain is an organ that requires high-energy that is powered by glucose; certain professionals suggested that the cells in the brain that are responsible for maintaining a person's self-control use up glucose quicker than it is being replenished. They performed a study with dogs where the dogs that were obedient and were asked to resist temptation showed lower blood glucose levels compared to the dogs that did not need to use self-control.

They found similar patterns in humans during scientific studies. The people who needed to use willpower in tasks were tested to have lower glucose levels compared to the participants that weren't asked to utilize their willpower. Moreover, replenishing glucose levels tend to help reboot a depleted willpower source in individuals that were depleted while drinking a sugar-free drink did not.

However, there is still evidence that suggests that a person's attitudes and beliefs can maintain the depletion of willpower. Different research and other colleagues found out that the people who felt the need to use their willpower (usually to please other people) were found to be more easily depleted compared to the people who are driven by their own desires and goals. These researchers, therefore, suggested that the people who are in better touch with themselves may be better off in life compared to the people who are often people-pleasing.

Some other researchers also studied how the effects of mood could affect a person's willpower. A study that took place in 2010 discovered that the group of people who believed that willpower is a limited resource were more likely to have willpower depletion. However, the group of people that did not believe that willpower can be depleted didn't show any symptoms or signs of willpower exhaustion after using their self-control. During the next stage of the same study, the psychologists manipulated the participants' subconscious beliefs by getting them to fill out a biased questionnaire unknowingly. The group that was manipulated to believe that willpower is for a fact a limited resource exhibited symptoms of willpower depletion/exhaustion while the group that believed that willpower was not depletable didn't show any signs of declining self-control. With this being said, your mindset regarding your willpower will play a huge role in whether or not you will perceive it as 'running out.'

Improving Your Self-Control With Money

People who want to grow their wealth are the people that need to have the most self-control with their money. To do this, you need to be able to tap into your self-control and willpower. A ton of research has been developed recently to explain the numerous elements of willpower. Many professionals that study this area of self-control to this with one goal on their mind. They are about these types of questions: If willpower is a limited resource, what can we do to conserve it? How can we strengthen willpower?

One effective tactic for maintaining willpower is simply to avoid temptation. In the marshmallow study, children were given a choice of being allowed to eat one marshmallow right away or having to wait an undefined period of time to have the opportunity to eat two marshmallows. They found that the kids who started at the marshmallows during the whole time were found to be less likely to resist the treatment compared to the kids who shut their eyes and refused to look, looked away, or created a distraction for themselves. The technique of out of sight, out of mind, works with adults as well. In a recent study, researchers found that office workers who kept unhealthy snacks such as candy in their desk drawers consumed it less compared to when they would put the candy on top of their desks at eye level.

A technique called "implementation intention" is another helpful tactic that helps improve willpower. These intentions are usually in the form of "if-then" statements that aid people in planning for situations that are likely to disrupt their goals. For instance, a person that is monitoring their consumption of alcohol may tell themselves before entering a drinking part that is anybody offers them an alcoholic drink. They will request a plain soda with lime. Research has found that amongst adults and adolescents, implementing solutions will increase self-control, even if people already had their willpower depleted by other tasks. People that have a plan ahead of time allows them to easily make decisions at the moment without needing to draw upon their bank of willpower resources.

This research suggests that people who have a bank of willpower that is limited raises a few troubling questions. Are people destined to fail if they are being faced with too many temptations? The answer is not necessarily. Many psychologists have the belief that a person's willpower cannot be ever used up completely. Instead, people often have stored some backup willpower that is being saved for future demands. Those reserves are only available for the right type of motivation, allowing them to accomplish things even when their willpower has seemingly run out.

To demonstrate this idea, a researcher found out that individuals who had their willpower used up 'completely' continued to be able to accomplish self-control tasks when they were being told that they would be compensated well for their actions. He concluded that having high motivation can overcome weaken self-control.

Will power can also be controlled in the first place to be less vulnerable to being completely depleted. Psychologists often use an analogy to describe will power as being similar to a muscle that will tire out after a lot of exercises. However, there is another element to this analogy. Although muscles will tire due to exercise during the short-term, they become stronger when regularly exercised over the long term. Just like physical exercise, self-control can become stronger when a person exercises willpower.

According to one of the earlier experiments that supports the idea above, the researchers asked participants in the study to follow a two-week guide to improve their moods, track their food intake, or improve their physical posture. Compared to the group that didn't need to exercise self-control, the participants who had to use their willpower by performing heavy willpower exercises were not as vulnerable to the depletion of self-control in a follow-up study. In another set of research, this researcher found that smokers who exercised willpower for two weeks by avoiding sweet foods or squeezing an exercise handgrip, found more success when it comes to not smoking than other participants who performed two weeks of tasks that didn't require any self-control.

Other researchers have also discovered that using your willpower muscles can help a person increase the strength of their self-control over some time. Some researchers in Australia did a study where they assigned participants to a physical exercise program that lasted two months; this is a willpower-required routine. In the conclusion of this program, the participants that finished it scored better when measuring self-control compared to the other participants who were not assigned the exercise program. The participants that did the program were also reported to have been smoking less, eating healthier food, drinking less alcohol, improving their study habits, and monitoring their spending habits more carefully. Regular exercise of a person's willpower using physical exercise seem to have led to an increase of will power in components of their daily lives.

The research findings regarding how glucose levels are tied to willpower depletion suggest a conceivable solution. A person that is maintains their blood sugar by eating regularly and often may help their brain replenish their storage of willpower. Those who are dieting aim to preserve their willpower while calorie reduction may be more effective by eating frequent and small meals compared to skipping out on entire meals like lunch or dinner.

All this evidence, founded from studies of the depletion of willpower, proposes that people making resolutions for the new year is the worst approach possible. If a person is running low on willpower in one specific area, it often reduces their willpower in all of the other areas. Focusing on one goal at a time makes more sense. In other words, don't try to get into a healthy diet right away, quit smoking, and start a new workout plan all at the same time. A much better technique is to complete goals one by one. Once you have one single good habit nailed, people no longer need to use their supply of willpower to maintain that behavior. Healthy habits will eventually become a part of a person's daily routine and would not need to use the energy of decision-making at all.

There are still many questions regarding the nature of willpower that needs to be answered by future research. However, it seems like if somebody has clear goals, good self-monitoring, and does a little bit of practice, they can train their self-control to be strong when faced with temptation. Now, let's take a look at a research study on the relationship between a person's willpower and financial decision making.

Research Study: The Effect of Willpower on a Person's Financial Decision Making

The temptation of consuming in materialistic things like new shoes or a new car is a test of willpower that we have all experienced. Just like how unhealthy food options have become plentiful, the opportunities for impulse spending has grown as well. ATMs are on every corner, and the rise of shopping online only allows a person to spend all their money without having even to leave the comfort of their couch. Willpower depletion affects people's ability to choose healthier lifestyle options and also affects their purchasing behavior.

Professors from the University of Minnesota did a study that focused on impulse buying and willpower depletion. They showed the participants a silent movie with a series of words that appeared on the bottom of the screen. A group of those participants was asked to not pay attention to those words, which were a task that required the use of self-control. After the movie, the participants were asked to look through a catalog with products like cars and watches, and they wrote down the money amount that they were willing to pay for every single item. The participants that used self-control during the movie were willing to spend more money, about $30,000, while the participants who didn't deplete their willpower were willing to spend approximately $23,000.

In the next experiment, the researchers tested the spending behavior of the participants by showing them the opportunity to buy lower-cost objects like cups and decorative stickers. The group that had done self-control in the previous experiment expressed that they felt a higher temptation to buy those items. In fact, They purchased more items and spent more money compared to the participants who hadn't done the self-control exercise.

The task of making decisions financially can be much harder for impoverished people. Researchers conducted various studies in India to explore the relationship between poverty and will power strength. In one study, this researcher visited two different Villages, one that was poor and one that was richer. The researcher offered people an opportunity to buy a luxury brand name soap at an extremely discounted price tag. This item was a great deal in terms of cost, but it still showed that people who live in poverty had difficulty making financial decisions as such.

The participants in the study were told to squeeze a handgrip made for exercise, before and after the soap was offered to be purchased. The researcher found that the participants who had more money exercised the handgrip for the same amount of time prior and posted to the opportunity to buy that soap. However, they found that poor participants squeezed the handgrip for a smaller amount of time after making a purchasing decision. Their willpower was depleted. The researcher had concluded that it was likely run down by the difficulty of making that financial decision.

This research may sound depressing, but there is a silver lining. If impoverished people have a higher chance of using up their willpower, then it could possibly mean that lowering the number of hard decisions that they have to make every day to help prevent the depletion of willpower will give them the ability to make future decisions. A different researcher studied this effect amongst thanking customers in Southeast Asia. They offered customers the opportunity to open a savings account, but it comes with a catch. These customers would only be able to withdraw their funds after reaching a targeted saving goal or target date that they have decided for themselves. A year later, the participants that signed up for these accounts saved 82% more than the participants who had not opened the special savings account. When the decision to save money or spending money is taken away, it helps customers avoid failing at self-control.

All of this evidence collaborated to show that the people who are in the lower end of the socioeconomic spectrum are more likely to deplete their self-control resources. It's not that people who don't have money have less willpower than rich people; rather, the people that are living in poverty have to make more willpower draining decisions. This means that every decision they make, whether it is as simple as buying soap, will require self-control, which, therefore, dips into their limited resources of willpower.

Chapter 4: How to Improve Self-Discipline to Save Your Money

With your new understanding of self-discipline and willpower, I will now be teaching you step by step on how you can achieve strong self-discipline. This will help you make better decisions and improve your productivity-related to your finances. Regardless of whether it is your finances that you want to improve or just some areas of your personal life, self-discipline is the driving factor behind it all. Everyone faces difficult decisions when they are presented with temptations that are hard to resist. A person that is looking to eat healthier may struggle with their self-discipline when they are offered a hot fudge sundae. A person who is looking to gain some muscle mass may face temptation of wanting to sleep in rather than going to the gym. People that have stronger self-control often spend less time thinking about whether or not to indulge in temptations that are bad for their health. Instead, they are able to make better decisions for themselves more easily. They don't let feelings or impulses affect their decision making. They are always able to make level-headed decisions.

Here are ten steps that you can follow to master your self-discipline as it related to your financial management:

Step 1: Identify What Your spending weaknesses

Everyone has their own set of weaknesses. This could range from spending money on leisurely activities rather than saving it for future investment, or it could be as simple as choosing to play video games than to work on your business/side gigs. Regardless of what it is, it has a similar effect on everyone.

The first step to mastering your self-discipline is to acknowledge your shortcomings, no matter what they might be. People often try to pretend that their weaknesses don't exist in order to portray themselves as a strong person. This is extremely ineffective when it comes to self-discipline. The purpose of acknowledging your weaknesses is not to make yourself feel bad; instead, it helps you recognize what they are and will help you plan in advance to overcome them. Acknowledge your flaws; it is impossible to overcome them until you do this.

Step 2: Eliminate Your temptations

Once you have acknowledged your weaknesses, you can now move on to step two, which is to remove your temptations. Just like we mentioned in step one, everyone has their own set of weaknesses, and it can range from small things like an unhealthy snack to something that hinders your productivity, like playing a video game for hours on end. By understanding what your weaknesses are, you can make accommodations for yourself that will help remove some of those temptations.

For example, if somebody is looking to lose weight and get fit at the gym, but they know that their weakness is that they always eat chocolate after dinner every night. Their temptation removal, in this case, would be not to buy any more chocolate that they keep around in their home. By not having chocolate in the home, they would be unable to fall into the temptation of eating it, which will hinder their progress of getting fit. However, this does not mean that they will never be able to eat chocolate again. This only means that they can indulge in their favorite snacks when they have achieved a certain portion of their goal. Rewarding oneself is important to self-discipline, as well.

Step 3: Build a Financial Plan With Clear Goals

In order to continue strengthening your self-discipline, a person must have a clear vision of what goals they are trying to accomplish. They must also have an understanding of what success means to them. If a person doesn't know where they're planning to go or what accomplishing their goals are, it is easy for them to lose their way or to get sidetracked.

Make sure the goals that you are setting have a clear and concise purpose. For example, don't use goals like "I want to be rich by the next five years." This goal is too broad for it to have a strong meaning. Instead, you should make a goal that is quantifiable like "I am planning on saving $20,000 by the end of this year". Then, when you have a quantifiable goal, you can make a plan that makes sense for yourself. For example, a person can plan to save $2,000 each month for the year to hit their goal of saving $20,000 by the end of it. They can break down these goals even further, and figure out where in their budget they can save money or how they can make more money to accomplish that goal.

Step 4: Train Your Self-Discipline Every Day

Self-discipline is not something that people are born with; it is mostly a learned behavior. Self-discipline is just like any other skill that people may be looking to grow; it requires repetition and lots of daily practice. Similar to going to the gym, the more you work out your muscles, the bigger and stronger they will become. Changes do not happen overnight, instead to strengthen your muscles and to grow them; it will take at least several weeks for a person to be able to see their progress. The effort and focus that training self-discipline requires can be extremely tiring.

Step 5: Build Simple and Healthy Habits

To strengthen self-discipline, you need to work on instilling a new habit, which can feel very intimidating at first, especially if you are focusing on the entire goal all at once. To avoid this daunting feeling, keep it very simple. Break your bigger goal into smaller doable ones. Instead of trying to accomplish one huge goal all at once or to change all of your habits, focus on doing just one thing consistently, and exercise your self-discipline with that one small thing. For example, if you are somebody that is looking to get into better shape, start by exercising for 10 to 15 minutes per day. Instead of trying to go to the gym for 2 hours every day, which can be very daunting, start with a smaller goal in mind first. By taking baby steps, you can get your mind used to that habit and slowly increase the amount of time that you spend at the gym. Eventually, once you feel like that goal has become a habit, you can then begin to focus on other small goals and keep building up words from there.

Step 6: Implement a Healthier Lifestyle

Eating well affects people more than they think. We learned in the earlier chapters that glucose levels play a big role in a person's brainpower, which controls a person's willpower. The sensation of being hungry can cause people to feel angry, annoyed, and irritated. This feeling is real, and everyone has felt it before and often has a huge impact on a person's willpower. Research has found evidence that having low blood sugar weakens a person's ability to make good decisions.

When a person is hungry, their ability to concentrate suffers a lot, and their brain doesn't function as optimally. This can cause you to spend your money on unhealthy items like junk food. Therefore, a person's self-control is likely to be weakened when their body is in this state. To prevent this, make sure to be eating small meals constantly to prevent yourself from feeling that annoying hungry feeling that causes people to have a lapse in judgment. Since exercising willpower takes up a lot of energy from a person's brain, make sure to keep fuelling it with enough glucose so that the brain can keep functioning at an optimal level.

Step 7: Change Your Views on Willpower

We learned in the earlier chapters that a person's point of view or their beliefs can create a buffer of how long it takes to have their willpower drained completely. Although most researchers believe that there is a limit to how much we can tap into our willpower, they also found that the people who believe that there wasn't a limit had a bigger will power stockpile. If a person believes that they have a limited amount of willpower, they probably will not be able to surpass those limits. However, if a person does not place a strict limit on themselves, they are less likely to use up their willpower stockpile before meeting their goals.

Step 8: Create a Backup Plan

Many psychologists use a famous technique that helps with boosting willpower called "implementation intention." This technique is where you give yourself a plan when you are faced with a potentially difficult situation. We used this example earlier, if a person is trying to reduce the amount of alcohol that they drink and they know that they are going to a party where they will be asked if they want to drink alcohol, instead of always asking for a beer like they normally do, they will instead ask for a plain soda with lime.

Step 9: Reward Yourself When You've Achieved

Just like anything else in life, it is necessary to give yourself a break and to reward yourself. Give yourself something to look forward to by planning an appropriate reward when you accomplish your goals. This is not much different from when you were a little kid, and you got a treat from your parents for showing good behavior. When a person has something to look forward to, it gives them the extra motivation that they need to succeed.

Step 10: Forgive Your Mistakes and Move On

Even if a person has all the best intentions and the most well-made plans, sometimes they will fall short when practicing self-discipline. Avoiding failure altogether is impossible, and we should not build a mindset around that. Everyone will have their ups and downs, their successes, and their failures. The key to overcoming the failures that you will face is simply to keep moving forward. If you stumble on your journey of self-discipline, instead of giving up altogether, acknowledge what caused it, learn from it, and then move on.

Money-Saving Tips

On top of building better habits to help you spend money responsibly, there are other ways for you to save money. In this section, I will be walking you through a few money-saving tips that anyone can follow to increase their savings account. Keep in mind; these tips are only helpful if you put them to use. You may have bad habits surrounding what you buy and how you buy. Use the self-discipline techniques you learned earlier in this book to put these money-saving tips into practice.

1. <u>Cut down on grocery costs</u>

If you don't already have a grocery budget, you need to start one now. First, start calculating how much you usually spend on groceries every money. If you're the average American family, you are likely spending around $650 every money on groceries. That is a lot of money. You can actually cut down that spend by half. It's very easy just to grab a bag of chips or a box of cookies that a) cost a lot of money, and b) are not healthy and won't fill up your stomach. Save money on grocery costs by planning meals each week and assessing the products that your pantry already contains before heading to the grocery store. Alternatively, grocery stores now offer online orders so you can pick your groceries online before going to pick it up. This will help get rid of temptations that you get when you get into the store.

2. <u>Cancel your automatic subscriptions</u>

You likely have multiple subscriptions such as Netflix, Spotify, or gym memberships. Assess which ones you do NOT use on the regular (regular means you're using it several times per week).

Cancel it, and if you feel as if you really can't go without it, you can re-subscribe.

3. <u>Borrow items, don't buy them</u>

If you require an item that you know you'll only use occasionally like a tree trimmer or camping tent, borrow it from someone you know rather than buying a brand new item. If you must buy an item, look for the same model or same item on a second hand buy/sell site. If you don't use this item on the regular, sell it back via those websites. This way, you are almost always breaking even every time you buy something 'new.'

4. <u>Ask for discounts/barter</u>

If you're going to a well-established business such as the movie theatre, you may not be able to barter the price of your movie ticket. However, you should ALWAYS ask if they have any discounts, deals, or coupons available at the moment. Sometimes, if you have a membership with a gym or your AAA, they may have hidden discounts. If you are shopping at a local farmer's market, be sure to barter. Usually, they always offer discounts for people who want to buy in bulk.

5. <u>Lower your cell phone bill</u>

Believe it or not, many people's cellphone bills exceed $100 per month. Try to cut that down as much as you can. Save money on areas that are not completely necessary, like cellphone data, phone insurance, or additional warranties. If your current provider cannot offer you any discounts or simply refuse to, look into switching providers and watch how quickly your original provider changes their mind! In addition, you can switch your monthly plan to pay as you go plans. That way, you aren't spending unnecessary money if you don't use your cellphone as much.

Chapter 5: How to Build Healthy Money Habits

Those who are successful at building sustainable typically share common habits. These habits help them live a more well-rounded life that improves their productivity, discipline, and overall drive. Healthy money habits are not only habits related to how you spend/save your money. It is also the habits that you implement into your overall life that will affect the way you view your money and your relationship with it. In this chapter, I will teach you the 10 habits that successful money managers have so you can begin implementing them into your life. Also, I will also teach you about how habits are formed. Understanding the science behind how habits are formed will help you better understand what you need to do to solidify these habits into your life. Let's first start with learning about how habits are formed.

How Does a Person Form New Habits?

Why is it so hard for people to stick to their new good habits for a certain amount of time before they give up and go back to their old ways? The huge problem in this, especially with old habits that have been there for years, are the neural pathways that have been imprinted into people's brains. This happens on a biological level. These neural pathways are responsible for linking up the neural networks in a person's brain to perform a specific function like pouring a cup of tea in a certain way, walking up the stairs, or smoking a cigarette.

These neural pathways created by our habits help us reduce the energy needed for the conscious processing power in a person's brain by automating certain behavior. By doing this, it allows a person's mind to focus on other things rather than the habitual tasks that they have done a thousand times. This automation function came from the beginning days of human life as a part of our DNA. It allows us to have a mind that is efficient and can be used for more important tasks rather than mundane things in our lives. The main difference between successful people and those who aren't is that they haven't mastered the art of forming these neural pathways for tasks that are beneficial towards your professional development.

In most scenarios, the things that often hold people back from building good habits are the mundane things we are used to repeating. More often than not, people tend to have automated more bad habits than good habits, which adds negative value to their life that causes them to achieve their goals slower, if at all. Since the cause of this is the neural pathways that get ingrained deeper and deeper over time, it makes it harder for people to break their bad habits or even form good ones when all of the bad ones are constantly getting in the way. However, if you can try to ingrain the next following habits we will be discussing into your life, you will find that strengthening your self-discipline may become easier. Again, these things don't happen overnight. Keep in mind that habits take a long time to break and to form. It is important to start small and build new habits slowly as neural pathways do not get ingrained overnight. It will require repetition for many weeks to months before your brain automates these tasks. Discipline is very necessary for the initial stages of building a habit; however, if done correctly, it will be able to pay off for the rest of your life. Let's take a look at ten habits that all financially stable people have, that you should start building to become more successful.

Habits That Financially Stable People Have

The habits that I will be teaching you will range from incorporating exercise to increasing your perseverance. Wealthy people face all types of adversity, so having higher energy levels and a stronger mindset will help you overcome the obstacles that will be thrown at you. Let's take a look:

1. Time Management

If you are looking to build wealth for yourself, you must maximize your use of time. Spending most of your time doing things that don't add to your future will only slow down or stop the process of you gaining the success that you want. To build wealth, whether that's by developing and honing a new skill or if it's managing your finances better, you must be able to manage your time properly so you can put the effort in the right places properly. An average person has to work at least 40 hours per week, all hours outside of that are limited, so time management is crucial.

When people can properly manage their time, they will begin to have room to do the things that matter. Mainly, they must make room to do the activities that they need to achieve the goals that they have set. For a person to achieve their long-term goals, they have to break it down into smaller daily goals that may not be the most urgent but are still very important. If a person does not have good time management, they likely cannot even get the most urgent things that they need to get done in a day, let alone achieving goals that don't require immediate urgency.

To effectively measure if certain things are urgent, non-urgent, important, not important, you need to take a moment to think about whether or not the action that you are doing is not 'urgent but important' or 'not urgent and not important' or 'urgent and important.' The things that fall into the 'not urgent and not important' category are known as things that are time-wasters. This includes things like browsing social media on your phone or binge-watching your favorite Netflix series. Things that fall into the category of 'not urgent but important' are likely the short-term goals you have set for yourself. Although they don't need to be urgently completed, they are still important for your self-growth. Most of the tasks that you will be doing to move you closer to becoming a millionaire will fall under this category. Things that are urgent and important are likely deadlines or any responsibilities that you have to complete for your work.

A person's ability to strengthen self-discipline comes from their time management abilities. Some of the most successful people in the world are incredible time managers because, rather than using time as a detractor, they use time as a benefit. Everybody has the same amount of time in a day; we shouldn't waste it. Start managing your time by categorizing the things you need to do in a day with the categories I gave you above. Start by doing the things that are both urgent and important, then move on to the things that are non-urgent but important. Leave the things that are both not urgent or important to the end of the day when you have completed all the other things. By doing this, you are maximizing your time for activities that are most beneficial to your growth.

2. <u>Persistence</u>

When it comes to managing your money and becoming successful, grit and persistence are crucial. No amount of self-discipline would ever be complete without the presence of persistence. Persistence is a type of habit that helps us not to give up even when we are faced with failure. Persistence is what helps us get back up on our feet to keep trying even when we do fail. Persistence plays such a huge role in self-discipline that without it, achieving self-discipline is probably impossible.

You might be wondering why that is. This is because achieving our goals is not an easy thing to do. It is really hard. Getting discouraged is easy and something that happens to everyone along their journey. In addition, the act of giving up requires less energy in comparison to being gritty and pushing through, even if it's a task that may cause pain in the process before any pleasure is returned. Successful entrepreneurs did not get to where they are by giving up when faced with hardships.

However, this hardship that is required to achieve any goals is simply something that you have to persevere through. We all have to understand that some of the most successful people in the world have experienced failure numerous times. Failure is simply a part of life, and rather than avoiding it and not pursuing your goals at all in fear of failure, we should learn to persevere and push through even during the hardest of times. Without failure, we wouldn't be able to reach our goals.

There are a variety of ways that a person can go about instilling perseverance as a habit, but the best and most effective weight is to come up with the reasons why you want to do the things in life that you aim for. If the reasons behind your goals are strong enough, they can motivate you so you can get through anything. The next time you are faced with an obstacle, rather than falling back onto your automatic bad habits of giving up, try something new and push through it. Get creative and problem solve; this will take you closer to achieving your goals!

3. Exercise

Not only is exercise one of the cornerstones of living a healthy life in general, but it is also one of the most important habits to build within all people. It is a fundamental habit to help a person's life be filled with positive habits and be rid of the bad ones. A person that is truly able to discipline themselves has to instill the habit of exercise into their everyday routine. As you may already know, there are endless benefits when it comes to exercise. This is something that is talked about not only by psychologists but medical experts as well. Even though exercise is such an important component of a person's life, not everyone actually makes it a priority. Why is this?

As our lives get increasingly busy in the modern-day, everyone is caught up with trying to get all the things that they need to get done and are often busy running around completing errands and fail to incorporate exercise into their routines. People have a bad mindset when it comes to exercise. These people think that they won't be able to build it as a habit because they have "too many other things to do." Most people are wrong to think that. There are ways to incorporate exercise even if their day is jam-packed from beginning to end. In fact, it will help you become more productive and efficient when achieving goals.

When people think of exercise, they may automatically think of a minimum duration of one hour performing an intense weight-lifting session at the gym, a one-hour long, expensive spin class, or a one-hour yoga class. If that's what they are thinking about then yes, indeed, the people that have busy lives may not be able to incorporate the time to get to their exercise class, the time it takes to complete the exercise class, and then get to wherever they need to go after that. However, exercise doesn't necessarily have to be a formalized session that takes a long time. It can simply be getting some sit-ups, push-ups, or some jumping jacks in the morning before you head to work. It can also be you choosing to walk to work instead of taking the bus, or it could be a brief walk around your neighborhood park after dinner.

Begin by starting to build exercise habits in your daily routine by starting with an easy 10-minute walk or just doing some sit-ups and push-ups right after you wake up. Attempt to do this for one week and then increase the amount of time you spend on that session for the next week. Keep up with this pattern, and soon enough, you will have a healthy amount of time every day that you set aside to get your exercise in, and this is when it will become a full-blown habit.

When you can implement exercise as a keystone habit of your life, it can help you increase self-discipline and can also improve other areas of your life. First of all, exercise is extremely effective in reducing stress levels and pain because it causes the brain to release feel-good endorphins and neurotransmitters like serotonin and dopamine. Secondly, exercise helps increase the oxygenation and blood flow of body cells, which is responsible for helping boost the immune system and fighting off diseases. Lastly, exercise increases a person's ability to focus on a present task due to the increased activity in the brain, which allows us to live a life with more discipline.

4. <u>Healthy sleep cycle</u>

According to the theory that we learned earlier in this book about willpower, we learned that willpower requires energy from the brain, which gets its energy from glucose levels and rest. Based on this theory, it is safe to assume that sleep is directly connected to how the brain is able to acquire energy. When a person doesn't get enough sleep, their brain spends most of its energy focused on just keeping your basic body functions up and going. This does not leave much energy for a person to spend on exerting their willpower, practicing self-discipline, or even simply just remembering their self-discipline. Ensuring that you get the right and a healthy amount of sleep is a crucial requirement for accomplishing anything. When a person doesn't get the right amount of sleep, it affects one's ability to focus, their judgment, their mood, their overall health, and their diet.

When people suffer chronic sleep deprivation, such as insomnia, things go from bad to worse. Many research studies have found evidence that people who don't get enough sleep on a day to day basis are put at a higher risk of catching specific diseases. Not sleeping enough also has a significant and negative effect on a person's immune system. This can cause a person to frequently catch colds or cases of flu that cause them not to have the ability to go to school, work, or get anything effective done. It is necessary to keep your body in good health to be productive. Constantly being sick or feeling unhealthy will simply make it harder for you to complete tasks that help you achieve your goals and may cause you to give in to temptation easier than if you had a healthy body and mind.

For most adults, get at least six hours of sleep every night. Ideally, you should be sleeping 8 – 10 hours per day. Avoid eating or drinking anything with caffeine in it before you go to bed to avoid it, affecting your sleep cycle. Make a note also to avoid ingesting a large number of toxins during your day like; cigarettes, alcohol, drugs, or prescription medicine if avoidable.

If you can improve sleep, you will gain extraordinary benefits. Benefits include; longer periods of staying focused and being more disciplined, minimizing pain and inflammation, reducing stress, improving memory, sharpening attention, improving your work quality, limits your chances for accidents, and helps you avoid depression.

5. Healthy diet

Eating healthy is as important as exerting perseverance. If you are not eating a healthy diet, you are actually preventing yourself from reaching your full potential. What a lot of people don't realize is that our human body spends a huge portion of its energy digesting and processing food.

Healthy foods that you should be eating more of are raw fruits and vegetables. Raw fruits and foods give us the biggest boost of energy for humans because they use less energy for the body to process and provides higher energy levels for us to use after that. This process is called an enhanced Thermic Effect of Food (TEF) or otherwise known as Dietary Induced Thermogenesis (DIT).

According to what we learned earlier in this book, the human brain uses up a large amount of glucose to keep it functioning. Therefore, the amount of energy that a person has is responsible for how focused they feel when doing work. When a person is focused, they can achieve their goals using less willpower and time than if they weren't focused. When a person is running on low energy due to consuming foods with empty calories, staying focused will be very hard to achieve. People will often waste a lot of time sitting around or 'resting' as they feel too sluggish and tired to work on achieving their goals.

One of the most commonly heard things is that breakfast is the most important meal of the day. Although breakfast is important, it is just as important to eat multiple times per day and not just only eating breakfast. By ensuring healthy meals every part if the day, start by actively planning your meals to avoid falling into bad habits. For example, if you are planning to eat five healthy smaller-sized meals per day, but you haven't prepared any of those meals, you are more likely to feel hungry and indulge in unhealthy conveniences like fast food. Prepare your five healthy meals beforehand by meal prepping to ensure that you don't fall into eating unhealthy conveniences.

The food that we put into our body can change the neural chemical makeup of the human brain. It also plays a huge role in a person's mind and body connection. Take some time to assess the foods that you eat throughout your day. Identify the meals where you often consume the unhealthiest foods. Make an effort to plan in advance so you can substitute those meals with raw, organic, and healthy foods.

6. Active goal setting

If your main goal is to build sustainable wealth, then you must actively set and adjust all smaller goals along the way that will help you achieve your main goal. Keeping your goals stagnant or refusing to break them down into smaller milestones will not only overwhelm you but can easily demotivate you.

Let's learn the difference between active goal setting and passive goal setting. Passive goal setting means you are setting goals mentally, which makes them passive because of the lack of details involved. It also means that a person hasn't properly defined their actual goal, which makes causes difficulty when it comes to tracking progress and identifying the tasks that need to be done to achieve that goal. On the other hand, active goal setting is the complete opposite of passive goal-setting. Active goal setting means writing out your goals and ensuring an important meaning behind it. Active goals are measurable and specific. To successfully create and make an active goal, you must build a plan towards achieving it. This includes breaking down your goals into smaller tasks and steps that are clear and achievable.

By implementing active goal-setting into your daily life, it ingrains the discipline in us because you are forced to give it direction. By breaking down your big goals into smaller daily goals, it helps people avoid distractions by only looking at the things that they need to get done in the present day. This way, a person isn't left constantly thinking about one large intimidating goal but not knowing how to approach it.

Active goal setting works by taking the first step in setting your long-term goals. If you currently have long-term goals, then you need to actively participate in daily, weekly, and monthly goal setting and planning. You have to play an active role in tracking your progress towards your goals and making changes in places where you feel like they aren't working for you. Rather than just saying that your goal is to become a successful entrepreneur, you need to start planning exactly what steps you believe will take you there.

My advice for you will be to take out a pen and a piece of paper and start writing down what long-term goals you have. Once you have some long-term goals written down, break it down into monthly, weekly, and daily goals. Simply start by accomplishing your daily goals, and when you reach the end of the month, assess to see if you have achieved your monthly goal through accomplishing your daily goals. If you haven't, look back on your daily goals and see if there's anything you can change so that you could achieve next month's goal.

7. Gratitude

Building a habit of gratitude may not be a habit
that you would think contributes to one success.
However, gratitude is an important feeling and
practice in human life that helps not only people
with self-discipline but is often used to help people
that are facing self-esteem and self-confidence
issues. A huge problem in our modern world today
is that we are constantly presented with millions of
mundane things that cause us to always be
wanting something more or something else. This
causes people to spend too much time thinking
about all the things that they want, and not enough
time thinking about the things that they already
have. Building a habit of practicing gratitude helps
people stop thinking about wanting the things that
they don't have and move forward towards
appreciating the things that they do have. When
people do this, they can begin to make changes in
their life that truly matters.

The effects of practicing and showcasing
gratitude are extremely crucial to fostering
success. It does everything from improving mental
health, emotional well-being, a person's
spirituality, gratitude is capable of so many things.
Practicing gratitude is an exercise that is
continuously used in therapy to help the client
move away from thinking about things that aren't
in the present and focus on being mindful.
Ultimately, gratitude helps people move away
towards a state of abundance and away from a
state of lack. When people live in a state of lack, it

makes it impossible for them to focus on achieving their goals and being self-disciplined. They spend too much of their mental energy and capacity worrying about the things that they don't have or living fearfully, to the point that they forget about the things that they do have.

The state of lack can also show up in someone as physical symptoms. This state produces a lot of stress because the brain automatically releases cortisol and epinephrine, which are the stress hormones from our brains. These hormones impact numerous systems within the human body. When someone is stressed, their immune systems, digestive systems, and reproductive systems are all affected. When this happens, you have to spend more time and energy recovering your body rather than using your resources to achieve your goals. Start by practicing gratitude by writing down ONE thing that you are grateful for in your day. This will help you put your mind at ease and to give you some more perspective about the world.

8. Forgiveness

Have you ever caught yourself feeling angry or impatient over the smallest matter? This is because of the large amount of convenience we are offered in our daily lives. A simple annoyance that occurs in your day can cause a spiral of negative emotions. For example, if you are in a hurry to get to work and you happen to be running late that day, the coffee shop that you normally stop at to get your morning coffee is taking forever to make your order. When you finally get your coffee, you realize that they had made your order wrong, but now you have no time to get it fixed. That one simple human error has sent you into a spiral of anger and annoyance, and you struggle to let go of it, and you find that it is still negatively impacting your whole day. This causes you to have spent most of your energy upset about the coffee shop that wronged you, and you don't have enough mental capacity to focus on other things like practicing your self-discipline. When people spend most of their days feeling the emotions of anger, regret, or guilt, they are creating more problems than they are with solutions. The emotions of anger and hate consume much more energy in a person's body compared to positive emotions like forgiveness and love. Forgiveness is something that can be learned. When people learn to forgive, only then will they be able to let go of negative things they have been holding on to.

If you aren't able to practice forgiveness in all areas of your life, to yourself and to others, you will have a hard time achieving true self-discipline. When an individual is constantly worried about how someone or something has wronged them, it makes it impossible for them to focus their energy on tasks and things that truly matter. If someone has hurt you in the past, start to try and learn how to forgive them. This does not mean at all that you have to forget about what they did to you altogether. Simply just forgive and let go of that negative energy and give it back to the universe rather than keeping it within your body. When we perform the act of forgiveness, we are actually letting go of the negative energy that inhibits our ability to practice self-discipline. If you want to master self-discipline, you have to get rid of sources that are sucking away at your mental energy. Holding on to negative emotions like anger is a sure way for your energy to be drained. While forgiveness might not seem like a discipline habit when you first look at it, it is an extremely crucial one to build in the process.

To start practicing your forgiveness habit, try to think of any people or situations that you are currently angry with. This can be someone that has wronged you in the past or a situation that affected you. Instead of just thinking about how it made you feel, try to put yourself in their shoes. What would be the things that you would do if you were in their situation? Make it light-hearted and try to find some humor in it. Instead of thinking about it as a situation that shouldn't have happened, try to think of a lesson learned. I know that it is very hard to forgive certain people, especially if they have hurt you or wronged you in life. However, it isn't until people can move on from feelings of animosity and hurt where their life actually begins to see some improvement.

9. <u>Meditation</u>

Similar to the effects of practicing gratitude, meditation is a commonly used technique to help people practice mindfulness in cases where they are suffering from feelings of anxiety and/or depression. Meditation is something that can be used to help put people's minds at ease. When people practice meditation, they take their awareness away from things of the past and the future. They should try and focus on the things of the present. When this happens, they can connect themselves to the universe, which also helps them with increasing gratitude.

When you are able to maneuver your mind to stay in the present moment, you will give yourself room to think about the tasks at hand and not predict problems of the future. By doing this, it plays into improving your time management and overall productivity.

There are many types of meditation. Some meditation focuses on mindfulness and some of which focus on love and gratitude. There truly are too many different types of meditation for humankind to keep track of. Still, the most popular and beneficial type that is used amongst many therapies and within self-discipline is mindfulness meditation. Contrary to common belief, meditation only requires ten to fifteen minutes and doesn't need to be for hours on end.

However, the hardest part of meditation is actually bringing yourself to do it. A person has to be able to keep their mind still and train it to stop wandering all the time. The trick behind mindfulness meditation is not to stop wandering thoughts altogether, but simply to acknowledge these thoughts and reroute yourself back to the present. There are many types of breathing techniques that can be accompanied with meditation to help with achieving mindfulness. You will have the chance to learn about using meditation in the next chapter.

Chapter 6: Getting Rid of Your Negative Mindset With Money

A common trend in those who are bad at managing money is the mindset that they have towards money. Typically, if a person has had bad experiences with money, such as poverty, then they may unconsciously build negative associations with money in their mind. When a person consistently has negative thoughts towards a certain subject or situation, they may develop what is called an 'unhealthy thinking pattern.' This is a common element that is used in Cognitive Behavioral Therapy to help people change unhealthy thinking patterns that they may have. Let's learn a little bit more about how Cognitive Behavioral Therapy can help you challenge the unhealthy thinking habits that you may have towards money.

Cognitive Behavioral Therapy is traditionally used to treat mental disorders, primarily anxiety and depression. However, many professionals now use it to help treat milder issues such as; self-esteem, overthinking, and negative relationships with specific objects/situations. Due to its long history and development, CBT is a practical and time-saving form of psychotherapy. CBT focuses on your here-and-now problems that come up in daily life. It is used to help people make sense of their surroundings and events that happen around them. CBT is very structured, time-saving, and problem-focused. These advantages are the reason why CBT is one of the most popular techniques when used to deal with mental disorders in our fast-paced modern lives.

In the present day, CBT works by helping clients recognize, question, and change the thoughts that relate to the emotional and behavioral reactions that cause them difficulty. By using CBT to monitor and record thoughts during undesirable situations, people begin to learn that the way they think is a contributor to their emotional problems. Modern-day Cognitive Behavioral Therapy helps reduce emotional problems by teaching individuals to:

- Identify any distortions in their thinking process
- See their thoughts as ideas rather than facts
- Take a step back from their thoughts to look at situations from another perspective

The new CBT model used in the present day is built on the relationship between thoughts and behaviors. Both can influence each other. There are three levels and types of thoughts:

- Conscious thoughts: These are rational thoughts that are made with complete awareness

- Automatic thoughts: These are the thoughts that move very quickly; you are likely not to be fully aware of their movement. This means that it's difficult to check them for accuracy. A person suffering from mental health problems may have thoughts that are entirely not logical.
- Schemas: These are the core beliefs and personal values when it comes to processing information. Our childhood and other life experiences shape our Schemas.

Using Cognitive Behavioral Therapy to Challenge Your Unhealthy Thinking Patterns

Take a deep look at yourself, do you feel like you have a negative relationship with money? If so, a lot of your decision-making related to money may be entirely dependent on the negative thoughts and feelings you have towards money. CBT is a great structure to follow to start taking a better look at what types of thoughts you have towards money and how you can change negative thoughts into positive and supportive ones. Let's take a look at the different unhealthy thinking patterns you might have in regards to money.

1. All or nothing thinking: This is otherwise known as 'black and white thinking.' You tend to see things in either black or white or

success or failure. If your performance is not perfect, you will see it as a failure.

2. Overgeneralization: You see one single negative situation as a pattern that never ends. You draw conclusions of future situations based on one single event.

3. Mental filter: You choose one single undesirable detail, and you exclusively dwell on it. Your perception of reality becomes negative based on it. You only notice your failures, but you don't look at your successes.

4. Disqualifying the positive: You discount your positive experiences or success by saying, "that doesn't count." By discounting all your positive experiences, you can maintain a negative perspective even if it is contradicted in your daily life.

5. Jumping to conclusions: You make a negative assumption even when you don't have supporting evidence. There are two types of jumping to conclusions:

    a. Mind reading: You imagine that you already know what other people are thinking negatively of you, and therefore you don't bother to ask.

    b. Fortune-telling: You predict that things will end up badly, and you convince yourself that your prediction is a fact.

6. Magnification/Minimization: You blow things out of proportion or inappropriately

shrink something to make it seem unimportant. For example, you beef up somebody else's achievement (magnification) and shrug off your own (minimization).

7. Catastrophizing: You associate terrible and extreme consequences to the outcome of situations and events. For example, if you are rejected for a date, it means that you are alone forever, and making an error at work means you will be fired.

8. Emotional reasoning: You assume that your negative emotions reflect the reality. For example, "I feel it so, therefore, it is true."

9. "Should" statements: You motivate yourself using "shoulds" and "shouldn'ts" as if you associate a reward or punishment before you do anything. Since you associate reward/punishment with shoulds and shouldn'ts for yourself, when other people don't follow it, you feel anger or frustration.

10. Labeling and mislabeling: This is overgeneralization to the extreme. Instead of describing your mistake, you automatically associate a negative label to yourself, "I'm a loser." You also do this to others; if someone else's behavior is undesirable, you attach "they are a loser" to them as well.

11. Personalization: You take responsibility for something that wasn't your fault. You see

yourself as the cause of an external situation.

12. All at once, bias: This is when you think risks and threats are right at your front door, and the amount of it is increasing as well. When this occurs, you tend to:
    a. Think that negative situations are evolving quicker than you can come up with solutions
    b. Think that situations are moving so quickly that you feel overwhelmed
    c. Think that there is no time between now and the impending threat
    d. Numerous risks and threats seem to all appear at the same time

By understanding these unhealthy thinking patterns, you will have the opportunity to interrupt the process and say, for example, "I'm catastrophizing again." When you can interrupt your own unhelpful thinking styles, you can readjust it to something more helpful. In the next section, we will be discussing some tips and tricks to help you challenge your own unhealthy thinking patterns. This is one of the main strategies within CBT.

Challenging Your Unhealthy Thinking Patterns

Once you are able to identify your own unhealthy thinking patterns, you can begin trying to reshape those thoughts into something more realistic and factual. In this chapter, I have categorized all the unhealthy thinking patterns with examples and what questions you should be asking yourself to develop different thoughts.

Keep in mind that it takes a lot of effort and dedication to change our own thoughts, so don't get frustrated if you are not succeeding right away. You probably have had these thoughts for a while, so don't expect it to change overnight.

Probability Overestimation

If you find that you have thoughts about a possible negative outcome, but you are noticing that you often overestimate the probability, try asking yourself the questions below to reevaluate your thoughts.

- Based on my experience, what is the probability that this thought will come true realistically?
- What are the other possible results from this situation? Is the outcome that I am thinking of now the only possible one? Does my feared outcome have the highest possibility out of the other outcomes?
- Have I ever experienced this type of situation before? If so, what happened? What have I learned from these past experiences that would be helpful to me now?

- If a friend or loved one is having these thoughts, what would I say to them?
- *Example: "If I invest my money, I will probably lose it all. Nothing good ever comes from my money, leaving my bank account."*

Catastrophizing

- If the prediction that I am afraid of really did come true, how bad would it really be?
- If I am feeling embarrassed, how long will this last? How long will other people remember/talk about it? What are all the different things they could be saying? Is it 100% that they will talk about only bad things?
- I am feeling uncomfortable right now, but is this really a horrible or unbearable outcome?
- What are the other alternatives for how this situation could turn out?
- If a friend or loved one was having these thoughts, what would I say to them?
- *Example: "If I started my own business, it would just fail anyway. There's no point in me spending the time and money to do this."*

Mind Reading

- Is it possible that I really know what other people's thoughts are? What are the other things they could be thinking about?

- Do I have any evidence to support my own assumptions?
- In the scenario that my assumption is true, what is so bad about it?
- *Example: "This financial advisor probably thinks I'm such a loser. I'm 31 and have less than $1000 to my name. I should probably just give up."*

Personalization

- What other elements might be playing a role in the situation? Could it be the other person's stress, deadlines, or mood?
- Does somebody always have to be at blame?
- A conversation is never just one person's responsibility.
- Were any of these circumstances out of my control?
- *Example: "My potential business partner seemed off today. It must be because they know my business will never be successful."*

Should Statements

- Would I be holding the same standards to a loved one or a friend?
- Are there any exceptions?
- Will someone else does this differently?
- *Example: "I should be saving every penny, no matter what."*

All or Nothing Thinking

- Is there a middle ground or a grey area that I am not considering?
- Would I judge a friend or loved one in the same way?
- Was the entire situation 100% negative? Was there any part of the situation that I handled well?
- Is having/showing some anxiety such a horrible thing?
- *Example: "If my business doesn't make at least $100,000 in its first year, then I've failed."*

Selective Attention/Memory

- What are the positive elements of the situation? Am I ignoring those?
- Would a different person see this situation differently?
- What strengths do I have? Am I ignoring those?
- *Example: "Yes, I've been very good at increasing my savings lately, but I still don't have my own business yet."*

Negative Core Beliefs

- Do I have any evidence that supports my negative beliefs?
- Is this thought true in every situation?
- Would a loved one or friend agree with my self-belief?

- *Example: "I never have enough money, every time I make money, it's already accounted for. There's no point in me trying to save since it never works anyway."*

Practicing Mindfulness and Meditation

Another area that causes people to have bad spending/money habits is their inability to be mindful of how they are using their money. When a person regularly practices mindfulness and meditation, it helps them better understand their thoughts and intentions. Thus, helping them realize when they are managing their money incorrectly. In this section, I will be teaching you about how you can use mindfulness meditation to become more aware of your thoughts and to understand better how you are spending your money.

Mindfulness is a type of meditation that is used as a mental training practice that requires you to focus your mind on your thoughts and sensations in the present moment. Your thoughts include your physical sensations, passing thoughts, and current emotions. Mindfulness meditation often utilizes mental imagery, breathing practice, muscle and body relaxation, and awareness of your mind and body. For beginners, it is recommended to follow a guided meditation to direct them through the entire process. If nobody is guiding you through this meditation, it is easy to drift away and fall asleep. That is not the purpose of meditation. When you become more skilled in doing mindfulness meditation, you will be able to do it without a guide or any vocal guidance.

The most original and standardized program for mindfulness meditation is called the Mindfulness-Based Stress Reduction (MSBR) program. This meditation was developed by a Ph.D. student who was a student of a famous Buddhist monk. This program focuses on helping the individual bring their awareness to the present and to focus on their own awareness. This meditation has increased in popularity and is not incorporated into medical settings to treat health conditions such as anxiety, negativity, insomnia, pain, and stress. Although this meditation is quite straightforward, professionals would recommend you to find a teacher or a program that can act as a guide when you begin. Most people are recommended to do this meditation for at least 10 minutes per day. If you don't have a lot of free time, that's okay. Even just a few minutes a day plays a huge role in changing your wellbeing. Follow these instructions below to get started:

1. Find a quiet place, and you feel comfortable in. Ideally, this is your home or a place

where you feel safe. Sit in something comfortable like a chair and make sure your head and back are straight and aligned. Try to release any tension you feel.

2. Begin to sort your thoughts and put away the ones that are of the past or future. Focus on your thoughts that are about the present.

3. Begin to bring your awareness to your breath. Focus on the sensation of air moving through your body when you inhale and exhale. Focus on this feeling. Begin to feel the movement of your belly as it rises and falls. Feel how the air enters through your nostrils and leaves through your mouth. Pay attention to how each breath is different.

4. Watch your thoughts come and go in front of you. Pretend you are watching the clouds, letting them slowly pass before you. It doesn't matter if your thought is a worry, anxiety, hope, or fear - when these thoughts pass by, don't ignore them or suppress them. Simply just acknowledge them calmly and anchor yourself by focusing on your breathing.

5. If you find yourself being carried away by your thoughts, observe where your mind drifted off to, and without judging yourself, simply anchor yourself by focusing on your breathing. This happens a lot with beginners, so don't be hard on yourself if

you drift away. Always use your breathing as an anchor.

6. When you are nearing the end of your 10-minute session, sit still for two minutes and bring awareness to your physical location. Get up slowly.

Chapter 7: The Importance of Goal Setting

Setting financial goals for yourself is a huge part of being able to manage your money successfully. Without any defined goals in place, it is very easy to spend money to satisfy your instant gratifications. The goals you set for your money must be something that you are passionate about and is realistic. For instance, 'becoming a millionaire' isn't typically defined as a person's passion. However, setting a goal of buying your first home in 5 years is something that you can be passionate about. In addition, a goal like this can be easily defined, whereas a goal of 'becoming a millionaire' is too broad and is difficult to break down into steps. In this chapter, you will be learning about how you can set goals for your money and how you can then break it a large goal down into smaller goals that you can work with on a daily/weekly basis. I will also be teaching you two strategies that will help you better define and achieve your goals. Let's get started.

Breaking Down Your Goals Into Manageable Ones

When a person is taking a look at a large money goal, such as buying their first home, it will feel overwhelming, and they likely won't know where to start. The only way to overcome it is to sit down and to assess what all the steps are in this goal and how you can incorporate that into a daily/weekly plan. When you have smaller and more frequent goals to work with, you can chip away at a larger goal. Simply just stating that you have a large goal of ABC is too broad and won't help you actually get started.

Start by just breaking down whatever that task is into littler parts and then focus on one at a time. If you find yourself still wanting to procrastinate after you've already broken it down, then break it down even more. You will eventually get to a point where the task that you need to do is so easy that you would feel very badly about yourself if you didn't just do it.

Let's use an example regarding filing taxes. As someone who is learning to manage their money better, one important task that you have to do is to file your taxes at the end of the year properly. Imagine that you are feeling overwhelmed as you don't even know where to begin when filing your taxes. You are also afraid that you may owe money to the government that you might not have. Here is how I would break down the large and broad task of 'filing taxes':

1. Research the best way to file taxes for entrepreneurs

2. Explore my options (either downloading software for DIY or going to a tax filing company)
3. Pick which option suits you best
4. Gather the documents that are suggested based on which option you chose in step #2
5. Follow the instructions given to you by the tax software or the tax professional

Suddenly that one large task of 'filing taxes' became much more manageable. Instead of thinking about filing taxes as one large unit, you are now starting with a simple google search of the best way to file taxes for beginners. From there, now you can make an educated decision on which method is easiest for you to proceed with. By taking things one step at a time, your mind becomes less overwhelmed. Do you see how this would also work with larger goals than just taxes? Having a step-by-step plan makes your goal seem less far-fetched and actually attainable. Now, I'll be teaching you about two strategies that will help you better define your goals, achieve them, and how you can develop new skills quickly to help you generate more income and success.

Strategies to Help You Better Set and Achieve Goals

The first strategy we will talk about is meditation. One of the most influential and inspiring things that humans can do is being able to visualize the things that they want to manifest and then actually making it happen. The power of the human mind is extraordinary, especially when it is coupled with mindfulness practices like meditation. Using meditation, a person can increase their ability and make heaps of progress towards the life that they want to create for themselves. As an entrepreneur, you MUST have a vision for your business. A weak vision will not suffice in this scenario; you must have a clear and defined vision of what you want your business to be.

Goal setting is the first action that a person needs to make in order to reach their goals. The purpose behind setting a goal is so that a person would be able to achieve their desired results. When a goal is set carefully with focus, momentum, action, and intention, setting and achieving goals is the first step a person needs to take in order to move from where they are not to where they want to be. However, they need to know where it is that they want to be. The "where" begins with a person envisioning it.

The first step to this is to start with imaging the end in mind and work backward (this is what we discussed in the visualization chapter. Many people mistake their goal for vision, thinking when the goal is actually the result. They will set a goal without thinking about what the goal will allow them to do, be, or have in the long term. In order for a person to make the most out of their goal-setting process, it is important to think about what quality of lifestyle they would want to achieve ultimately. For clarity, let's talk a little bit more between a person's vision and their goal.

A person's vision isn't something that needs to be created from scratch; in fact, it is something that already exists inside them. They simply need to get in touch with it. A person's vision is the big picture of their desired outcomes. It represents the most important things to that person and is often compelling, inspiring, exciting, and filled with many positive emotions. A goal, on the other hand, is different. A goal is very specifically designed that requires tasks that need to be completed to get to the thing that they want at the end of their journey. The downside here is that a person's goal may not initiate those positive emotions that become an inspiration. Goals act more like stepping stones on a path that will lead you to your ultimate end goal.

The most popular and effective way to build your goals is using the SMART goals format. You may have done or heard of this before at your workplace or while you were in school. SMART stands for specific, measurable, achievable, resources, and time. This helps you make sure that your goals are specific and concise, you have a way of measuring them, they are achievable goals, you have or have a way of getting the necessary resources, and you have a timeline in which you want your goals to be met.

By using imagery that is vivid and highly detailed, it is a very powerful way for someone to train their mind to go after the things that they want. Remember, when we discussed how athletes often use visualization to help themselves train? For example, famous golf athlete Tiger Woods has been using visualization to help train his golfing techniques ever since he was a teenager. Even the NBA star Michael Jordan used mental imagery to help get himself into the mindset that he wants to be in order to make his famous three-point shots. If professional athletes use visualization techniques, they can enhance their ability to be the best. You can also use visualization and meditation to help you achieve your goals.

Here are the steps on how you can use meditation to break down a large goal into smaller ones effectively:

1. Start by thinking of an area of your life in your mind. Choose a financial goal that you have been struggling with, or you would like to change.
2. Now start to imagine the best possible outcome that you would like to be living in regards to the area that you've selected. Imagine this 6 to 12 months from now. What is the reality that you are looking to

achieve? Try not to get caught up with any negativity or limitations; instead, just allow yourself to imagine and get carried away with your strongest goals.

3. Focus your mind on connecting with just one goal that you would like to achieve over the next three months. Make sure your goal is a good one and is as meaningful as possible. If you choose a goal that isn't meaningful or doesn't hold a lot of weight, the end result won't feel special for you. Make sure to choose something that is significant enough so that once you achieve this goal, you will feel a high sense of accomplishment and motivation for your next goal. Be sure to run your goal through the SMART acronym to ensure that it is a goal that is set up for success.

4. Now that you are starting to feel connected with the goal that you've set, try to imagine what your life will be like once you achieve the goal. Visualize a picture or movie in your mind and try to view it as if you are looking at it through your own pair of eyes. Factor in all the other sensory perceptions to try to imagine the most real and positive feelings. Where are you? Who is with you? What are the things happening around you?

5. Now, begin to step out of the picture or movie that you've imagined and begin to imagine yourself floating up in the air above where you are sitting now while taking that

imagery with you. Take a deep breath and as you breathe out, use your breath to give life to the image and fill it with intention and positive energy. Repeat this five times.

6. In this step, it is time to imagine yourself floating out into the future while imagining yourself dropping the imagery that you've created for your goal down into your real-life below you at the exact time and date that you've set for yourself to reach this goal.

7. Pay attention to all the things that need to happen between then and now and how it is beginning to re-evaluate itself in order to support you in achieving that goal. Visualize this process and all those events to make it feel as realistic as possible.

8. Once you feel like that step is complete, bring your awareness back to the present, and with your eyes still shut, start to think about what steps you will need to take in the next few days that will help you move closer to achieving your goal.

9. Take a few more deep breaths in order to ground yourself to the present before opening your eyes. Now, before you forget, write down a list of steps that you need to take in order to achieve your goal or begin to write down your experience in your journal, so you don't forget.

10. In this last step, you will focus on taking action and staying focused. Make sure that

you are doing something that brings you closer to achieving your goal on a daily basis.

Use this meditation and visualization technique once a week after you first complete the steps. By doing this once a week, it helps you continue to move forward towards your end goal and help you bring your vision into real life. Seeing is believing, so using your mind and meditation, you can create the best future that you have imagined for yourself.

Let's look at the second technique; visualization. Visualizing an action or a skill before actually performing it is nearly as powerful as physically performing that action in reality. Scientific studies have found evidence that people's thoughts actually produce the same instructions in their mind as it does with actions. This means that when somebody is mentally rehearsing or practicing something in their mind using the visualization process, it actually impacts the many cognitive processes within a person's brain that includes planning, motor control, memory, and attention perception.

In layman's terms, the way a person's brain is stimulated when they are visualizing an action is exactly the same as when they are actually performing it physically. Therefore, scientists can safely assume that the act of visualization provides just as much value as physically performing a task.

Many athletes in certain sports use the act of visualization to help themselves train before a competition. For example, in Olympic cycling, the cyclist will prepare for a competition by closing their eyes and visualizing the racetrack in their mind. They move their bodies while visualizing the way that they will travel through the racetrack to train their muscle memory and reflexes even further. This way, when they do begin to compete on the racetrack, they have already visualized themselves cycling through it using the strategies that they have been taught and visualized in their minds. This is a technique and training skill that many professional coaches teach their athletes to do.

When a person is visualizing, their conscious mind is aware that what they're visualizing is not real but is just a result of imagination. Consequently, a person's subconscious isn't able to differentiate the difference between what a person is thinking and what they are actually doing. In other words, a person's inner-mind isn't able to distinguish the difference between real life, a photo, memories, or an imagined future. Instead, the mind is under the impression that everything a person sees is real. This is proven by numerous brain scans that scientists have conducted over the years, where they discovered that there are no brain activity differences when someone is observing something in the real world compared to when a person is visualizing.

All of this evidence is extremely important because it points the theory that visualization can help people learn new skills and be able to reprogram and rewire their brains without having to perform physical actions. For example, if somebody is looking to increase their self-esteem, they can use the process of visualization by imagining themselves doing those actions before actually doing it in the real world. Same with if somebody is looking to make better decisions with their money, visualizing themselves saving money and refusing to give into instant-gratification will be helpful for when they actually are faced with these challenges.

Visualization is often used by athletes to improve their technique in their sport. However, visualization can also be used to improve mental and emotional skills to reduce negative thinking and anxiety. It also helps a person improve their overall self-discipline, which we know, is extremely important to those trying to become better money managers. By using the technique of working through scenarios in a person's mind can help them effectively require their brain in order to build new patterns, habits, and behaviors, which makes completing tasks in the real world far less anxiety-ridden. Due to this, bringing your visualizations to life will help you feel more at ease.

Four different visualization techniques help a person improve different areas in their life; they are; mastering new skills, healing your mind/body, achieving your goals, and creating a plan.

Technique #1: Master New Skills Fast Using Visualization

Visualization can be used to not only learn a new skill but to master it as well. Visualization is really effective in mastering new skills because due to how the brain is exactly the same when stimulated. Someone who is visualizing the skill has the same brain activity as when they physically do that skill. Let's take a look at a study that an Australian psychologist did that studied the effectiveness of visualization regarding a person's ability to do free throws in basketball.

This psychologist chose three groups of students at random who have never tried visualization before. The first group practiced the skill of free throwing for 20 days straight. The second group only practiced free throws twice, once on the very first day and once on the last day. The third group did the same. However, the third group spent half an hour every day visualizing themselves practicing free throws. If they had "missed" in their visualized free throw, they "practiced" getting it right the next time.

On the last day of this study, the psychologist measured how the participants improved using percentages. The group that got physical practice every day improved their free throws by 24%. The second group that only practiced twice did not improve at all. However, the third group who had practiced just as much did 23% better, nearly the same as the first group. At the end of this experiment, the psychologist published a paper that was about how most effective visualization happens when the visualizer is able to see what they are doing. In other words, the ones that practiced visualizing the free-throw actually 'felt' the basketball in their hands and 'saw' it go through the hoop and have heard it 'bounce.'

You can also use visualization to improve upon any skills you want to learn. Specific to you, think of a financial skill that you want to improve on. This could be saving money, entrepreneurship, or anything similar. Make sure that you try to utilize all your senses when you are visualizing yourself to do this.

Below are a simple 5 steps to how you can use visualization to do this:

1. Choose a skill that you are interested in mastering.
2. Identify what your real-world proficiency level is in this skill.

3. Visualize yourself doing this skill in as much detail as you can use all five senses.
4. Repeat this visualization for 11 days at 20 minutes per day.
5. Perform this skill physically and keep track of measuring your improvement. Continue visualizing while doing that skill in real life if you are not satisfied with the results

Technique #2: Creating a Detailed Plan Using Visualization

As someone who is trying to get better at money management, it is easy to feel stressed when thinking about your finances. Creating a plan of action for your main goal using visualization can help you relax and motivate you to take action. This technique is most effective if you use it before you go to bed so you can start planning the next day's work. However, you can use this technique throughout the day if you have 10 minutes of free time.

Below are three simple steps on how to do this:
1. Calm yourself down, and make sure you are feeling relaxed. Sit down as it will help you get some rest from whatever you were doing before.
2. Close your eyes and start to visualize which things specifically that you want to accomplish for tomorrow. Now, visualize those actions that you'd like to do in as

much detail as you can and then ask
yourself these questions below:

    a. How do I want to feel?

    b. How will I interact with others?

    c. What specific actions do I want to take?

    d. What do I want?

    e. What obstacles will I potentially face?

    f. How will I overcome obstacles?

    g. What do I want to achieve?

3. The reality here is that people are not able to predict all the things that might happen to them. When events happen unexpectedly, they can often ruin any plans that have been put in place. However, good planning isn't about planning around all possible obstacles, but it is more about adapting to the obstacles that life gives you. When you keep this in mind, you must affirm with yourself at the end of your session with "this or something better will come my way." By giving yourself affirmation, you are keeping your mind open to endless possibilities. This will result in you be more ready and okay with making adjustments when unexpected things happen to you.

This process is definitely not a foolproof plan. However, this visualization will help you envision possible situations that might happen. These scenarios will allow you to be able to make better decisions as you continue to work towards your goals.

Technique #3: Achieving Your Goals With Visualization

By using the technique of visualization for setting goals brings a lot of value, but this technique does come with one major drawback. The most popular form of visualization is goal setting. Most people have definitely used visualization pertaining to their goals at one time or another. However, this technique may not have worked for them due to one critical flaw.

This flaw is that when people are visualizing their goals, they only focus on visualizing their end goal and nothing in between. They see within their mind's a big and flashy awesome goal that's going to be rainbows and butterflies. Yes, they are experiencing this using all of their senses, but they simply open their eyes after the visualization feeling very inspired. However, this type of motivation is extremely short-lived because the next time this person faces an obstacle, it immediately deflates their motivation.

When this happens, people feel the need to visualize their goal again to create more motivation. However, because nothing happens every time they visualize their goal, their motivation doesn't grow either. In fact, every time a person hits an obstacle, and they try the process of visualization again, their motivation becomes weaker every time, and they start to lose more and more energy.

The mistake that these people are making is that they are nor properly visualizing their goals. They only see the destination, but they don't understand that achieving a goal takes much more than just that. Achieving a goal is part of a journey that is full of emotional highs and lows, wins and losses, and a journey of ups and downs. Due to this, these are the things that a person would also need to include in their visualization.

When a person visualizes their end goal, it is very effective in creating that desire and hunger. However, the proper way to use visualization is only to spend 10 percent of your time visualizing the end goal and spending the rest of the visualization time thinking about HOW you will achieve your goals and overcome challenges. In some ways, it's similar to the form of visualization planning that we just discussed.

A person's end goal helps keep inspiration running in the long term, but it is the journey that helps a person stay motivated in the short term. The way to maximize the time spent on achieving small goals to get to your end goal, you must visualize those as well.

Below are five steps that you can follow to achieve this visualization:

1. Get yourself to a quiet place and sit down and close your eyes. Start to visualize your end goal. Imagine yourself experiencing and living this goal using all five of your senses.

2. Slowly take a few steps backward from your end goal and start to visualize the process that you took that lead to you achieving your end goal. Imagine all the problems, and you faced that put you back. However, you can see yourself finding solutions to those problems. Continue visualizing until you are back to the present moment.

3. Now, move forward with time and visualize how you took on opportunities that helped you overcome your problems.

4. At the end of this visualization, take a few moments to send your future self some positive energy for their journey.

5. When you exit the visualization, emotionally detach from the outcome of your goal. The thing that can hold you back is if you are having an emotional attachment to a specific result. Instead, try to stay open-minded and be flexible for what's to come on your journey.

You can use visualization using those steps on a daily or weekly basis. Weekly sessions can be as long as 30 minutes, and you can keep your daily sessions shorter, so they are between 5 - 10 minutes. However, be sure that you are using your daily sessions to visualize the next steps of achieving your goal for the upcoming week. This will help you continue moving forward to reach your goal. After that, you can use your weekly visualizations using the five steps above.

Chapter 8: Side Gig Ideas to Increase Your Secondary Income

Generating a secondary income is a great idea to help counterbalance your expenses and to increase the amount of money you can save per month. In this chapter, we are going to be exploring numerous different side gigs that can be accomplished by working out of your own home! With the technology that we have in the present day, more and more jobs are emerging in the industry that allows you to make money without leaving the comfort of your own home. The only requirement for these remote side gigs is to have a decent computer and internet connection. That's pretty much all you need! Before we get started on the different types of side gigs in this chapter, I will walk you through some benefits from working from home.

1. Flexible Schedule

Having a flexible schedule is crucial to many people, whether they have kids to pick up from school or if you are also working a full-time job. Having a flexible schedule where you can work whenever you want/need allows you to not be able to miss important aspects of your life like our children growing up or possible work promotions at your day job. Having a flexible schedule will allow you to maintain your full-time job while allowing you to pick up other side gigs as well to generate more income. This will help maximize the money you make for you to increase your savings and speed up your investments.

2. Flexible Environment

The second best part about working from home is the flexible environment that you can work in. For instance, if you had to go on a work trip that's 6 hours away from your home, you can still get work done for your side gig to maximize your income. As long as you have a laptop that you can take with you and a decent internet connection, you are still making money.

3. No Commuting

Some people would go as far as saying that they would give up a percentage of their salary just to no longer have to commute anymore. Luckily, with work from home side gigs, you can do it from the comfort of your own home without needing to take public transit or drive your car to a workplace. This not only saves money in transportation costs, but it saves you a lot of time that can be used to do more income-generating work. Moreover, depending on where you live, commute times could be up to over an hour in each direction. That's over two hours per day that you could be spending on other income-generating tasks instead.

4. <u>Save Money</u>

If you have ever worked a job downtown or in a city before, you will have noticed that unless you had the time to prepare a lunch every day, you are likely spending at least $4 for a coffee or $15 for a subpar food court lunch. Having the ability to work from home allows you to make your own meals and drinks, which saves you hundreds of dollars every month. Believe me, if you were conservative with your money and spent $10 every day for lunch and $3 for a coffee, you are spending $13 per day on food and drinks alone. That's $65 a week and $260 a month! The $260 could easily cover a significant portion of your bills.

5. <u>More time to spend with loved ones</u>

Last but not least, working from home allows you to spend more time with your loved ones. If you are working a full-time job, you are likely someone who spends a lot of time working in an office or somewhere away from home to make ends meet. This has likely compromised the time that you can spend with your family. This is especially true if you are married and have kids of your own. Working from home can allow you to spend time with your family and even pull more of your weight in parental duties if you have kids to give you the work-life balance that you need.

Remote Side Gig Ideas

A popular remote side gig trend at the moment is the world of online stores. Let's start off learning a little about online stores, how they can be side gigs, and what some of the benefits are. Online stores are similar to popular e-platforms like Amazon and eBay. However, the ones that can be utilized as side-gigs are typically on a smaller scale where sellers can post items they've made or second-hand items up for sale. There are numerous amount of online store platforms that are extremely user-friendly and can help you make money by selling your old items or hand-made items.

The first benefit that comes with using online stores as your side gig is time. You don't have to invest a lot of time into it, all you need to do to get started on most of these platforms is to make an account simply, have a few sellable items, and you'd like to sell, make a post, and reply to the interested people. Yes, it's really that simple. However, you have to keep in mind that some items receive more attention from customers than others. For instance, Apple products or any type of decently new electronics tend to get a lot of online attention. These products do well on second-hand online platforms like Letgo, Craigslist, and eBay. Let's take a look at some ideas now:

1. <u>Dropshipping</u>

Dropshipping is a fairly new business model that people can use to run their own online store. Dropshipping is simple; essentially, you have your own online store with items of your choice to sell. You also have a relationship with a wholesaler that can sell your products at wholesale prices. Items that you could sell include watches, mugs, clothing, electronics, anything you can dream of really. Once a customer purchases an item from your store, you will then purchase your item from the wholesaler and have the wholesaler mail that item to your customer directly. With dropshipping, you don't actually have to hold any inventory in your home or make any items from scratch. For instance, if you have a Shopify store selling watches and your wholesaler sells you watches for $15 and you sell them to customers for $40, you are making $25 of profit for every watch. You also get the benefit of not having to pre-buy inventory, so you are minimizing the risk of producing a loss. What I mean by this is the traditional way to run an online store is to have an inventory for things, right? So let's stick with the same example, let's say you wanted to run an online watch business and you bought 10 watches for this season to sell at $15 each. However, by the end of the season, you only sold 5 watches at $40 each. This means that you spent $150 on your inventory and only made $200, that's $50 profit, with 5 watches that are now out of season. Dropping shipping allows you to minimize your risk by purchasing items and selling them as the orders come in, therefore, maximizing your profit. In the same example of watches, if you only had 5ordersr for that season of watches and you bought 5 watches as those orders came in, then you have made $$125 profit compared to the measly $50 profit. Platforms that allow you to utilize the dropshipping method are Shopify, Amazon, and Alibaba.com.

2. Print On Demand (P.O.D)

The third type of online store that you can run is print on demand (P.O.D) businesses. This is similar to dropshipping but requires your artistic and design abilities. What P.O.D. entails is that you are selling prints that you have designed. This could range from your paintings, drawings, graphic design, ...etc. You are then selling your designs printed on items of the customers' choice in the form of posters, phone cases, t-shirts, tapestries, and many other options. You can choose to only sell one form of a product like specifically phone cases, or you can sell your designs on any imaginable printable surface. This is ideal for someone who has a strong artistic ability to create designs. Depending on the popularity of your art, this can be a business that has an extremely high earning potential. The costs simply consist of the items that you want to be printed on (e.g., t-shirt, phone case) and a company to do the actual printing itself. For instance, if a printing company agrees to print your design for $10 on a t-shirt and the t-shirt costs $5, the total cost for your t-shirt + design is $15. If you are selling those shirts for $40, you are bringing in $25 of profit. Again, the great part about this is similar to drop shipping; you only have to pay for the cost of the orders WHEN you get the orders. This prevents you from having to hold a stock of different sized t-shirts with different prints which will cost you a fortune if the business is slow. You only need to pay for costs when you get an actual order, which will guarantee your profit. Platforms that support this type of online store include Printful.com, Printify.com, and Teespring.com.

3. Tech Support

This type of side hustle is not as popular as some of the ones we've talked about, but if you are someone that is very tech-savvy or works in the IT field in your day job, you can use your skills to make some extra cash. Platforms such as HelloTech match people with strong IT knowledge to people that need help with it. This can range from setting up their new computer to fixing a broken printer to diagnosing network problems in their home. If you work in a field where you have extensive tech knowledge and skills, you can also advertise those skills and services in your tech support freelancing. Depending on what level your IT knowledge is, you can get paid from $16 per hour to $53 per hour. Again, if you work in IT during your day job, this side hustle should be extremely easy for you, and you can not only make some extra money, but you can also add this experience to your resume and further build your technology career.

4. Editing and Proofreading

If you are someone that has good writing and editing skills, then proofreading and editing written documents is a great way for you to make some extra income. This is ideal for someone who may be in the field of writing and is looking for a way to increase their own writing skills while making money at the same time. There isn't a single platform that is dedicated to this type of work, but with a quick google search, you can find a variety of freelance proofreading and editing gigs. You can usually make around $200 - $300 per written document depending on its length, so just proofreading a few documents per month can significantly increase your monthly income. Moreover, you can look into freelance writing as well as there is growing popularity in hiring writers to write blogs, e-books, and articles.

Depending on which skills you plan on utilizing for your freelance work, the sites that I've provided above will vary inefficiency.
These are the websites you can consider for freelance work:

- Fiverr.com
- Upwork.com
- Freelancer.com
- Peopleperhour.com
- Writeraccess.com
- Freelancewriting.com

Other Profitable Side Gig Ideas

If you're not too picky about the remote aspect of your side gig, there are a large amount of other profitable side gigs that you can pursue. In this subchapter, I will be teaching you about various ideas that you can pursue to create secondary sources of income. Let's take a look.

1. Social Media

Social media is a relatively new way that you can begin to make money since it used to be used only to connect with friends, but now every business has multiple social media accounts- one on every platform. Companies and brands use these social media accounts to reach consumers and advertise their products. These days, there are advertisements on social media news feeds so that people see them as they are scrolling through their timeline looking at the people that they follow, as well as product placement in the posts of people with many followers like celebrities or models.

There are quite a few social media platforms, including Instagram, Facebook, Twitter, Twitch, Tumblr, TikTok, and so on. All of these platforms have the potential to make you money if you have a large following, which results in lots of likes on your content or millions of views on your videos. The best way to maximize your following is to cross over your social media accounts, advertising one platform on the other, so that your followers can follow you on every platform possible.

By using social media, the earning potential is pretty much unlimited, though you have to reach the level of social media celebrity to begin earning a lot of money. If you have around 10 thousand followers, you can begin to get partnerships with brands that will give you free merchandise or up to $150. The money really begins to flow when your social media following reaches one million followers. Then, you can begin to make 15 thousand US dollars for a single post! Any number of followers in between will give you some amount of money between $150 and $15 000. A big range, I know. But it really depends on the number of partnerships you have and the brands which are paying you to product place for them.

2. <u>Content Writing</u>

When it comes to side gigs in the realm of content creation, content writing is a great choice. This is fairly similar to the freelance writing gigs that we talked about at the beginning of this book. Still, the platforms within this category are specialized within the business writing industry. This includes any types of company blogs, LinkedIn articles, and e-books. In terms of flexibility, freelance writing work is extremely flexible since you can do it anywhere and at any time. The earning potential is fairly high, depending on what sorts of work you are qualified to write and how quickly you can write. The faster you can write, the more money you can make on an hourly basis. There are a few platforms that help connect content writers to businesses and people that require this talent. Problogger, medium, LinkedIn, and self-publishing books are methods where you can create income. Let's take a look at each of these platforms and methods and how you can utilize them to make money.

Problogger is a platform where it connects business-owners or individuals who require blogs written for their business to people who have experience doing blog-writing. Problogger offers services on starting a blog and creating content. The earning potential through this platform varies widely depending on the business demand. Most bloggers can make over $100 per month, but that's pretty low compared to other side gigs you can do to generate more income. In terms of flexibility, you can write blogs pretty much any time and anywhere as long as you reach the deadline required. There are new projects and blog requests posted daily for people to pick up as needed, but you do have to spend time sifting through the projects and figuring out which ones you are best qualified for. If writing is something of interest to you, you may be able to make more money writing e-books and articles for larger companies as their workflow is more consistent, and the rates are much higher.

Medium.com is a platform full of blogs and articles are written by amateurs and professionals for avid readers to go into and study their content. You can also write for medium.com to generate some income, but bear in mind that this stream of income varies widely and is on the lower end when comparing to other side gigs. It has high flexibility as you can essentially write about whatever you want, whenever you want, and you get paid monthly. If you have experience or a particular interest in writing content of all styles and topics, this may be a side gig that is right for you!

3. <u>Ridesharing</u>

Ridesharing is probably the most popular form of side gig available on the market right now. Working as a rideshare driver is a common and great way to make extra money as you can build your own schedule, and drivers average anywhere from $11 per hour to $29 per hour depending on what time of day that they decide to operate. Companies like Uber and Lyft are great platforms to get started with if you already own a vehicle and a valid driver's license. Not only is this method a great way for you to make an extra few hundred dollars a month, but you are also helping out people who need a ride. In fact, this side gig has gotten so popular and has brought in so much income that some people treat this side-gig as their main job. If you are someone that's busy with your work during the daytime, you can add a second source of active income by providing rideshare services on evenings and weekends. If you put an extra 10 hours a week on your evenings and weekends to do this, you can make anywhere from $110 - $290 per week. That is an extra monthly income of $440 - $1160. Depending on where you live as well, you pay less tax working as a contractor, so you actually bring in more money when it comes to tax and net income ratio.

Uber is the original player in the rideshare game and shares a very similar platform to Lyft. As long as you have a decently modern and clean car, you qualify to drive for Uber. You can build your own schedule simply by turning on your Ube app when you are ready to drive and turning it off when you are finished. There are also other ways to make more money, such as making your car nice with refreshments to generate more trips and driving during surge times where prices are higher. The flexibility in this type of work is very high, as you can literally work at whatever time you want. The only downside to this is that you have to be there physically, so you don't get the luxury of staying at home to work like other remote jobs.

Lyft is Uber's biggest competitor, and in terms of business model and platform, they are virtually the exact same. They do pay slightly different rates, but the difference is very small, and most people don't notice. Many drivers will drive for both Uber and Lyft to maximize the amount of business they get. The qualifications are the same for Lyft, where you need to have a decently modern car that is clean and in good condition to qualify. Other than that, you can clock in and clock out whenever you like. Both Lyft and Uber drivers make a percentage of what the platform charges the passenger. This means the faster and more rides you can get done, the more money per hour you are making. By any means, make sure you are still driving safe, but you could maximize your income by driving passengers in a timely manner. Keep in mind that ratings also matter. Based on your service and driving ability, passengers can give you a score from one star (poor) to five stars (excellent). This affects the number of passengers you get matched with and could make or break the business flow for you.

4. Renting Your Car

Another way that you can make a side gig out of your car is to rent your actual vehicle. It's exactly what you're thinking; you are essentially acting as a car rental company but with your vehicle only. This is a great passive source of income as you don't need to do anything besides confirming your customers, and you receive money from them using your car. Unlike ridesharing gigs like Uber and Lyft, you don't need to put in the hours to generate income, as long as your car is in decent shape, you can make money just by letting someone else use it temporarily. You can make good money by renting your car out if you are someone that doesn't use it a lot. Platforms such as Getaround, Turo, and Hyrecar pay you money to rent out your car just like any car rental company would, and you pretty much get paid for doing nothing at all! Average car renters make anywhere between $500 - $800 per month renting out their car. If you rent it out 100% of the month, you will make more money compared to only renting it 50% of the time. The model of your car makes a difference too, so if you have a fancy car like a Tesla, you can make a premium.

At the moment, it seems like Turo is the most popular platform in terms of car rentals, so that is one platform you can look into if you are interested in renting out your car. This platform also comes with a nice feature where you could get an estimate of how much your specific make and model of car can make for you. This is ideal if you want to have an estimate of its income before diving right into this type of side gig. With its increase in popularity throughout major cities, especially those with high tourism, you can make some serious cash by just letting someone drive your car for a few days! Not only does this help you make some extra cash if you are currently financing or leasing your car, but you can also use this money to help break-even with your purchase. Two birds, one stone!

Getaround is a similar platform to Turo that offers the exact same services. It does not have the same feature as Turo with the estimation calculator, but you could consider cross-posting your car into multiple car-share websites to maximize the number of times your car can be rented. The earning potential is highly dependent on what type of car you have, and the demand in your city but most car-renters report making anywhere from $500 - $800 per month.

HyreCar is an interesting platform as it is a combination of Turo and Getaround mixed with Uber and Lyft. Its services are specialized towards people who don't have a car but want to pursue rideshare jobs. HyreCar allows people to rent Uber/Lyft qualified cars for them to use Uber and Lyft to make money. This is an option for you as well in terms of side gigs if you don't have a car, you can rent a car starting from $25 per day and use it to generate income through rideshare or food delivery services. If you DO have your own car, then you can make money by posting on HyreCar and renting it to someone else. Again, if renting out your car is an option you are looking to pursue, cross-posting on these sites will help you generate the most business. Remember that renting out your car is a passive income, it allows you to do something else to make more money as a more primary and active source of money.

5. Food Delivery

Another very popular side gig these days that you can do with a car or some means of transportation is food delivery. Services like UberEats, Foodora, and Doordash frequently employ a team of food delivery people to pick up food from restaurants and deliver it to the person who ordered it. This type of side hustle originally started with delivering food from established restaurants but now has evolved into delivering everyday items like groceries, over the counter medicine, and alcohol. If you own a vehicle or a bicycle and enjoy roaming through the city you live in, you can sign up and make some money doing so. This is in no way a passive source of income, but it is a second active income that you can add to your earnings. These couriers have reported that they make around $12 - $20 an hour. If you dedicate an extra 10 hours of your week to this side hustle, you can make an extra $120 - $200 per week, grossing at $480 - $800 of extra monthly income.

Food delivery is a fantastic side gig if you don't have a car but have another means to deliver things quickly (e.g., electric scooter, motorbike, bicycle). If you have a car that you can use, but it is not modern enough to qualify for rideshare services like Uber and Lyft. It has the same flexibility as driving for Uber or Lyft as you can clock in and clock out whenever you like. It's earning potential is lower than ridesharing platforms, but the qualifications are much less compared to it. Nowadays, food delivery services have broadened their services to delivering other household items as now, so the business is rapidly growing in this department.

Platforms that offer this type of food delivery service include UberEats, Foodora, Doordash, and Skip the Dishes. Different platforms offer different rates and payment structure, but they all generally follow the same business model. The driver will get a notification using the app with a delivery that shows how much they would make. They can either accept or reject the offer based on the amount. Customers can also decide to tip before the delivery and after the delivery based on the courier's timeliness and attitude.

6. Tutoring

Tutoring is an amazing side gig that could bring in a significant amount of income. You can find these opportunities through independent tutoring companies or through other platforms like Wyzant and GlassGap. Tutoring can range from school subjects like math and science all the way to teaching languages. English teaching is a growing side hustle that makes enough money for someone to live on full time. Platforms like VIPKid pay their online English teachers anywhere from $17 - $22 per hour. The beauty of teaching English online is that you don't even have to leave the comfort of your own home, and you can choose which hours work for you. Meanwhile, tutoring can be done online or in-person, depending on which company you work for. If you are tutoring for a high school student, the average tutor gets paid anywhere between $30 - $40 per hour. Just by doing 10 hours of it a week can bring you $300 - $400 per week of extra income, that's $900 - $1600 per month.

Tutoring can be done in person or online, depending on your preferences. Online tutoring is more flexible as you can do it from your own home, but numerous tutoring companies in most cities hire tutors on an hourly basis to meet the needs of students. Depending on what your education level is, you could tutor students from the levels of elementary school, high-school, and post-secondary school. The higher level the education is, the higher you will get paid on an hourly basis. You can take a look at some in-person tutoring opportunities by looking them up based on where you live. If there are a lot of high schools or well-known universities in your area, the chances are that there are a lot of businesses that are looking to hire tutors for various subjects.

The above options are highly dependent on where you are located, so you can spend your own time researching about which options you have. Let's talk a little about online tutoring. Online tutoring is essentially the same as in-person tutoring except for the fact that you are doing it over video conferencing rather than sitting face to face. With online tutoring, the possibility of subjects widens even more. Now you have different options to teach multiple languages, the most popular being English, and other subjects that may be different from what local schools are teaching. Some of the most well-known tutoring platforms include tutor.com and pearson.com.

7. Music Lessons

If you are someone that has strong skills in music, this will qualify you to teach music lessons online or in your local music stores. Teaching at local music stores or finding clients on your own can generate an income between $20 - $30+ per hour. This is a very good income in comparison to most side gigs and is in a field within your passion.

Depending on whether you find clients through working at a music store or a teaching agency, you can host lessons in your home to increase flexibility. Doing in-person music classes tend to make a bit more money than doing them online. Again, you must consider the flexibility factor as well. If you require a lot of flexibility, teaching music online is a better option, but if you have an open schedule and a means of commuting to your students, then teaching in-person is a better option as you can make more money per hour.

When it comes to finding music teaching jobs in-person, do some research on your local music stores. Most music stores have a teaching department where they offer classes for a range of different instruments. You can simply walk in and introduce yourself with a resume and see if they have an opening, or you can go on their website and see if they have an application page. If you want to do this independently, you can put up an ad on your local buy/sell trade groups and offer your services. Finding your own clients will generate you the most income out of all these options as you don't have to give a portion of it to the company that employed you. Moreover, you can choose to host your music lessons in your own home to increase flexibility.

Chapter 9: Entrepreneur Ideas to Invest and Grow Your Money

Did you know that the average household in America has about $15,000 in credit card debt? Thanks to the spending culture that the Western world has fostered, people tend to spend money that they don't have through the use of credit cards and loans. Side hustles are a great way to make extra money to pay off existing debt and to begin building a savings account that you can use to generate more money in the future. In our modern world, other businesses have created numerous different platforms that help match people with certain skills to the type of work that requires it. Thanks to these platforms, about 10% of people have their own side hustles in our present day. In this chapter, I will be teaching you about the earning potentials of starting your own low overhead business venture versus utilizing side gigs. The most popular type of low business venture at the moment is a consulting/coaching business as it essentially has very low overhead costs, minimal equipment/material costs and can be tailored to whatever your skillsets are. Let's begin by taking a look at the earning potentials of a coaching/consulting business compared to other types of side businesses.

Earning Potential of Side Gigs

Before deciding whether pursuing side gigs or your own coaching/consulting business is better for you, you must analyze which of these two options has the highest earning potential for your individual profile. An important part of properly pricing your coaching business is to get a good grasp on what your earning potential is as a coach and how it compares to other side businesses. If you have the skill to start another side business that has a higher earning potential than a coaching business, then you might want to consider that option first as it is more suitable to your individual knowledge and skills. For instance, there is a multitude of different side hustles out there, ranging from rideshare services to vacation rentals to teaching to personal training. These side hustles, similar to a coaching business, has the potential to earn you an extra income of $500 - $4000 per month.

For instance, if you were to start a rideshare side business using existing platforms like Uber and Lyft, then you are already guaranteed clients as that's the platform's job to match you with people that need a ride. This is a quicker way to gain side business income while still working your full-time job. Rideshare drivers can make anywhere between $110 - $290 per week working part-time, which is an extra monthly income of $440 - $1160. In the next subchapter, you will learn what the earning potential is of a coaching business and will be useful for you to use to compare it with other side hustles that you may be interested in. Another example would be running your own vacation rental if you have an extra property or an extra room in your house/apartment. Rooms and units can be rented from $50 per night to $250 per night, which brings you a weekly income of $150 - $750 if you rent a space in your own home from Friday – Monday.

When starting a coaching business, it is important to keep track of how much time you are spending on it so you can divide out your revenue and profits per hour. Let's say you needed 10 hours of work to jumpstart your coaching business (e.g., getting a website/social media built, advertising, business development), and you managed to get yourself your first two clients. Since coaching sessions are usually one hour in length and may happen 1 – 3 times a week, you need to divide out your profit with how many total hours you've put into it. For example, let's pretend that your two existing clients agree to three coaching sessions per week for an open-ended amount of time. They may only need one month of coaching in total, or they may need several years, but they are playing that by ear.

Here are the numbers for this example:

10 hours (setting up the business)
2 Existing Clients (3 sessions per week)
$150 per session (1 hour)

This means that in your first week of coaching your clients, you have made ($150 x 3 sessions x 2 clients) $900. This sounds like a lot, but if you divide it out by the amount of time you actually put in, your revenue per hour is only $56 per hour. Of course, you have to keep in mind that the initial 10 hours that you've put in to get your business going likely is a one-time thing, but you do have to factor in the hours OUTSIDE of the sessions where you are scheduling, managing, and developing your business.

In other words, what I'm saying is that you must do these calculations before dedicating a generous amount of time to your business. If there are other side hustles out there that don't require such a large amount of time and pays more than $56 per hour, you may want to consider those options too. If you are interested, you can look into these following types of side hustles that can make you an extra income on top of your coaching business.

Earning Potential of a Coaching/Consulting Business

Now that you have a good understanding of what those side hustles can bring in terms of another source of active or passive income, let's talk about our main topic – the earning potential of a coaching business. If you are thinking about starting your own coaching business in the first place, you probably want to know how coaching compares as a career during these unstable times of the economy. The best part about this is that coaching is gaining a great reputation as a profession, probably because of the uncertainties in our economy, forced career changes, and drastic efforts made by businesses to make their operations more efficient and productive during the midst of numerous financial challenges. In terms of statistics, the coaching industry in 2012 brought in a revenue of $2 billion spread amongst approximately 50,000 coaches.

You may already know that coaches set their own rates and their rates tend to differ a lot. Some coaches may charge $25 per hour, while some may charge $300+ per hour. After coming out from a certification program, the standard hourly rates for certain coaches can be anywhere from $100 per hour to $150 per hour. The biggest differentiating factor between coaching rates is determined by the type of coaching that you are doing. Although there are numerous different types of coaching, the industry is generally divided into life coaching, business coaching, and executive coaching.

A recent study on the coaching industry found that the average income for coaches who worked full time was over $80,000. For coaches who did it part-time, it brought in income of around $25,000 per year.

Benefits and Drawbacks of Starting Your Own Coaching/Consulting Business

With your new knowledge of coaching/consulting businesses, it is important to learn the benefits and drawbacks that come with running one. Besides only learning about the different types of side hustles and coaching businesses and their earning potential, learning the nitty-gritty details of it is important when it comes to making decisions about any side gigs that you are interested in pursuing. Let's take a look at the benefits and drawbacks of going this route as your method of generating more income.

1. Benefit #1: Your Coaching Business Can Give You An Advantage In Your Career

We talked about this a little bit when we were learning about the different types of side hustles you can do. When you begin to work on other projects that people are paying you for outside of your main job, then you become growing your skills at that job more than others around you. For instance, if you are a teacher or an education professional, building and running your own coaching business can improve your teaching skills and overall experience, which puts you at an advantage compared to your peers.

Moreover, having a coaching business will challenge you to learn new skills. Although you may be a teacher for a certain subject, starting your own coaching business that enables you to teach other subjects will give you experience in them, which can help you get future career advancements.

2. Benefit #2: Your Coaching/Consulting Business Will Give You The Opportunity To Network With More People

Have you ever heard the saying, "it's not about what you know, but who you know?". This saying holds a lot of truth in the professional world. Often, employers would pass up a perfectly qualified candidate over someone that they know personally or came highly recommended by someone they know. This makes the art of networking extremely important regardless of what industry you're in. A solid recommendation can make the biggest difference between you finding a great job or no job at all. Coaching businesses are great in this way as depending on what type you do, you get to meet various people from various industries and allows you to connect with them and build a relationship. For instance, if your coaching business is to specialize in the corporate field, you are given the opportunity to meet your clients face to face and have a conversation with them. If your day job at a bank, you could likely meet people within the same field or from different banks that could give you a lead into better opportunities. The more people you talk with, the more opportunities begin to show up in your life. People who are referred to companies are statistically 54 times more likely to get the job compared to someone who applied online.

3. <u>Benefit #3: Coaching Businesses Are Effective In Creating Extra Income</u>

We all know that the main reasons that people take on side hustles or build their own coaching business are to create an extra stream of income. If you are lucky, your side hustle was already your passion project, but you realized that you could make some good money off of it. If you are someone who works a steady schedule and you feel like you still have some extra time left over in the week to do something productive, picking up a side hustle would be perfect for you.

For instance, if your day job was a graphic designer at a design firm, you may want to build your coaching business around targeting other artists. Although many graphic designers don't make a ton of money compared to other careers in technology, you can increase your income by building your side coaching business. This coaching business can be targeted towards other people you know in the industry that may be struggling with jumpstarting their careers, or it could be targeted towards people that you have never met. Regardless, career coaches make an average of $100 per hour for their sessions, so simply doing five sessions a week can increase their monthly income by $2000.

4. <u>Drawback #1: You Can Easily End Up Neglecting Your Day Job</u>

Depending on what your regular job and type of coaching business are, if your business is more interesting and is becoming profitable, you may easily find yourself spending your day job working hours on coaching business. Trust me; I've been there. Make sure you are clearly differentiating your hours between your day job and business in order not to neglect your main source of income. Of course, if your business becomes lucrative enough, you can consider switching your coaching business to your main source of active income, but until that point, I would make sure that you aren't jeopardizing your main source of income.

5. <u>Drawback #2: Running Your Own Coaching/Consulting Business Can Add More Stress To Your Life</u>

You may already be expecting this to be one of the drawbacks of running your own coaching business, but it is one that we need to talk about. You may be used to simply going to your day job every day and then coming home to do leisurely activities. You have the freedom to spend your weekends; however, you want. You have to consider that when you decide to pursue your own coaching business that there will be days where you come back from a long day at work and have to do urgent tasks for your business, such as emails, scheduling, or following up with your clients. You will also have to do extra paperwork or management duties like doing an extra set of taxes when tax season rolls around, or you may have to purchase the correct insurance for your business.

For instance, if your coaching business is targeted towards women that work in sales and a large finance company has just launched their corporate diversity program, then you may feel the need to jump on this opportunity to reach out to them to pitch your services. You may be feeling extremely drained coming back from your day job, but you know that this call is one that you have to make otherwise other coaches will be snatching up that opportunity before you. This can add a lot of complexity to a person's life because they may have to begin sacrificing their own leisurely time in the moments they need it most in order to have a chance to grow their business.

6. <u>Drawback #3: Not All Coaching Businesses Are Worth Your Time</u>

Before diving right into running your own coaching business, you have to know that not all side business ideas are worth your time. Depending on what type of coaching business you're the most qualified for or interested in, you have to make sure that the profit you're bringing in makes sense based on how much time and effort you are putting into it. For instance, before you jump into starting any business, think about how much time one task would take you (e.g., 1 hour, 2 hours, 3 hours) and figure out how much you're being paid for it ($50 $100? $200?) and divide the money by the number of hours required to find out how much you would be making hourly.

A good example would be if you are a general life coach, and you have a potential client that only wants one session with you to start with. They feel that one session will be 'enough' for their needs. For life coaching, you charge $100 per hour, and this client lives 45 minutes away and wants you to meet them at a coffee shop near their home. If the session is one hour long and it will take you 45 minutes to get there and back, you are spending a total of 2.5 hours on this client. When you divide

$100 out by 2.5 hours, you are actually making $40 per hour. If this is the case, you may want to reevaluate your specialty in a coaching business (e.g., is life coaching really the best coaching business for me? Can I make more money if I had a more niche specialty) or you may want to turn down the client and offer them a package of multiple sessions and explain why one session won't be enough. Either way that one session of business is likely not worth your time, and you have to make sure you are making these calculations to ensure that you are accepting the appropriate businesses for your goals.

Tips for Starting Your Own Coaching/Consulting Business

If you're wondering where to start with building your own coaching/consulting business to generate extra income, this subchapter will help you figure out the most important areas that you should determine first.

1. Establishing Your Specialty

It is important to figure out what type of coach you want to be and have the skills for. For instance, if you have a background in sports, it doesn't make much sense for you to be a corporate coach. You would probably make a better athletics coach or life coach. This seems like common sense, but this is a mistake that a lot of new coaches make is trying to be every type of coach in order to cater to more demographics. Their mindset is that they should never give up a potential client, so they sell their services to anybody who is interested. Coaching is an exploding industry at the moment, which means that numerous new coaches are entering the industry that you have to compete with. The more specialized you are and the better ability you have to differentiate yourself from the competition, the more success you will see in coaching.

Even if your niche is in the business or executive field as a coach, you can still specialize in your services even further. When coaches don't have a specific specialty, it is hard to pitch your coaching services to corporations or people that are interested. However, if you do specialize, you can pitch your services around producing a specific outcome such as increasing sales, retaining top talent, or developing leaders. By specializing yourself not only in a specific industry but a specific result in that industry, you will differentiate yourself from competitors. For instance, if you are a business coach focused on the Technology area, you don't have a lot to pitch about your services besides that you can help those who work in the technology field. However, if you were a coach that specialized in increasing sales in the technology field, you will begin turning a lot of heads, specifically the companies that are trying to sell technology-related products. By establishing yourself as an expert, you will gain plenty of new business, referrals, and repeat business as people tend to want to work with those who understand what their needs are and can produce tangible results.

2. Capitalizing On Writing And Speaking

If you are looking to become a coach and also have strong writing and speaking skills, then you likely already have a specialty. Not many people feel like they can be a good writer, so this strategy is genius on its own. Offering writing and speaking services is an incredible way to build your credibility and build a bigger audience in order to make more money. Some people may take the approach of writing books, but you could accomplish the same, if not more, by writing successful blogs. The theory behind this is to try to position yourself as a leader in your specialization. When you do this, you sort of become the 'go-to' person in your industry. Results from this are that when an organization or a person faces the same problem that you focus on, you are the 'go-to' person that they seek for help. Moreover, you can also make money on selling your writing, so that is a great way to add a source of passive income on top of this active income.

If you don't exactly know where to begin with writing, you don't have to worry too much. You can get a writer to help you get your thoughts together, or you can hire a ghostwriter to write your blogs or books for you. The main idea here is to be able to deliver your unique and valuable ideas to the market and to be able to get your brand out to your target audience. By doing this, you begin to build a strong connection with your audience; therefore, they already know you are reputable before you go in with your pitch. Building a sense of trust in your target market is crucial when it comes to building a successful coaching business.

3. Diversifying Income

As you may already know, coaches do a whole lot more than just coach. Coaches that make a ton of money through their profession likely have other products and services that are a part of their portfolio. Start thinking about what other services you could offer to your clients. This could include group coaching, physical training, consulting, online classes, and assessments. Like we mentioned before, additional products like a book or a blog can help create other sources of income. There is a lot of truth to the famous saying of "don't put all your eggs in one basket." The more services you are able to offer to your client base, the more revenue you can potentially bring in. This way, if one stream of service fails, you are still making money from your other streams. Just like any other type of business, the more time and effort you put into it, the more money that you will make.

Relating back to our first example (where set up time was 10 hours, and there are 2 existing clients), a way to increase your profit per hour is to diversify your income. We just talked about adding other sources, such as offering products like books or a blog. These products are a great way to create a passive source of income that will increase your profit per hour without you having to put in any extra work after the initial start up time. Let's say you are choosing to write a book on your coaching specialty. You can make this easier and less time consuming by hiring a ghostwriter to write your ideas for you. If the start-up cost of your book was $3000 and you are selling your book for $50 a copy, you easily break even by selling 60 copies. As you grow your client base, you can sell these books to your clients, or you can target a whole other market that may bring you new clients, as well. This way, once you break even with your 60th copy, every other book you sell is adding to your hourly profit. If you sold 100 copies of your book while still only having your original two clients at 3 sessions a week, your hourly profit has increased to $181 per hour.

This is why identifying different streams of active income and passive income is extremely important. You ideally want to have multiple sources of passive income so you can increase your hourly profit even if you are not actively putting in the work. Whether your passive profit is generated by your coaching business or by a different side hustle, this is extremely important as active income can be capped at the maximum hours you can work a week while passive profit cannot.

Different Types of Coaching/Consulting Ideas

Within this popular and new industry, there are different types of coaching that consumers are interested in. If you have a special technical skillset, consider building a consulting business with that. Examples of this include; IT Consulting, HR Consulting, Accounting Consulting, ...etc. For others that don't have a technical skillset, and you are interested in starting your own entrepreneur journey within the coaching realm, consider the following types of coaching:

    1. <u>Corporate Coaching</u>

Corporate coaching is also known as executive coaching is a popular service that large organizations require when they see growth in their business. Often times, corporate coaches offer their services to large businesses to help teach and educate their employees in important areas like sales, leadership, and team building. These services include face to face coaching from the executive level all the way to the front line level, training programs, team coaching, and they can also build customized coaching programs depending on the type of business.

The reason why businesses hire so many corporate coaches is that they are looking to solve a specific problem and need the coaches to help mold the employees to generate those specific results. Coaching can be specialized in a specific outcome, such as increasing sales, minimizing downtime, talent retention, or building more effective teams. In a 2011 study, coaches that worked with large companies made $325 per hour while mid to small-sized company coaches made about $235, and life coaches averaged about $260 per hour.

The truth of the matter is that large companies can afford to pay a premium for coaching, and they do it regularly. You can make as much as a corporate coach as a life coach that charges more, but most of the time, executive coaching pays much more than small business coaching or life coaching. As a corporate coach, you can sell more coaching options such as customized programs, assessments, training, and coaching services. You also can increase the number of billable hours due to the number of people in a company there are to coach.

2. Career Coaching

Career coaches are focused on helping people that are seeking career advice. These coaches use a very solution-oriented approach to help these people define, redefine, and achieve their goals that are related to the professional objectives of their current working situation. For example, a career coach can help people figure out what type of job they're looking for next in order to grow their careers. They are also specialized in giving people advice based on what their current working situation is. They could be executives, employees, or freelancers. Regardless, career coaches help these people develop skills like leadership, stress management, self-confidence, interpersonal skills, and conflict-management skills. The target market for this type of coach could be a new-grad that has just finished their degree and is looking to get their career started for the first time. Consequently, it could be an experienced executive that's 30 years into their career but is looking to either grow it further or to make a dramatic shift. Regardless, the target market for career coaches are simply people that are looking to make a change in their career to hit new or different goals.

The great thing about career coaching is that you are not only limited to an individual or small group clients. Career coaches actually have the option of opening up their business to target big corporations that may want to help their employees and executives grow with the company. When career coaches are working with a big organization, they help them with employment-related issues, staff training, role transitions, and general development. Most career coaches work independently by finding individual clients and such so they can also reach out to the entrepreneur market full of people that may be looking to start their own business just like the career coach themselves.

There isn't one specific way that a person can work towards being a career coach as career paths differ greatly from person to person, but there are some similarities that stand out when it comes to the career path of a career coach. A typical career coach normally has started their career in or has significant experience working as someone in Sales & Business Development, Employment Consultant (Recruitment, staffing, HR), and Customer Service Representative. These types of jobs typically build a good base for the person that is looking to become a career coach as you are exposed to reaching and measuring goals/sales quotas and have experience working with people from diverse careers and experience levels. Again, just because you have never worked as an employment consultant or in sales does not mean that you are not qualified to be a career coach. You could've had a very successful career in IT and want to focus your coaching business around helping other people in IT hit their goals and reach their full potential.

Let's dive into some of the primary responsibilities of career coaching. Career coaching is a highly diverse field, and as we talked about above, these coaches can work outside, within, or for an organization. Depending on what the clients' needs are, the career coach's responsibilities, tasks, and services will differ accordingly.

3. Life Coaching

Life coaches help their clients get a clear vision of how they want their life to look like on a day to day basis and help them make the necessary changes in order to achieve that goal. Life coaches help their clients overcome any life obstacles they may be facing and help them change aspects of their life or even make a big shift in their life in order to help them achieve their personal and professional goals. The coach that is working with the client normally has the mindset of understanding that the client already holds all the answers within themselves regarding the changes that they are looking to make, the coach is there to help them slowly gain clarity on what those answers are. The coach can take on individual clients, group clients, or corporate clients where they work on restructuring the company.

A life coach almost acts as a sculptor who is looking at a statue (that is the client) and sees the potential for what they can do and help them work away at achieving it. Life coaches utilize specific skills and strategies that help the client envision the life they want and helps them define who they are. In addition, life coaches help their clients create a detailed plan, action steps, and holds the client accountable for completing those action items. The coach typically uses a lot of soft skills like active listening, observing, question-based coaching, and motivating to run the majority of their sessions. Like I mentioned earlier, this is different from a therapist or a counselor as coaches do not analyze a person's past or do any type of mental health counseling. The principle of life coaching is based on the theory that the client has their own ability to determine their goals and then achieve them. The coach is simply there to help them see their own potential and guide them in achieving it. Everything that a life coach does is presently based on achieving something in the future.

Like we talked about earlier, within these specialized types of coaching, you can specialize even further.

When it comes to life coaches, here are some specializations that you could consider for your business:

- Relationship Coaches
- Personal Coaches
- Small Business Coaches
- Life Balance Coaches
- General Life Coaches

4. Business Coaching

A business coach focuses on helping a business owner to assist and guide them to run their business by clarifying the vision of their company and how it aligns with their personal goals. Alternatively, business coaches can help people who are looking to start their own business (entrepreneurs) and help guide them to follow the best business practices and aid them in creating a vision for what they want their business to be. In simpler words, business coaches follow a process to help grow a business from it's present state to where the client wants their business to be.

An important part of business coaching is for the coach to help the client understand that any company vision and story is completely theirs to create. Business coaches don't help their clients by creating their business stories and visions for them; instead, they help them discover what exactly their vision is and make a plan for them to execute on. The main role of a business coach is to introduce concepts, tools, and processes to their clients that help them grow their organization and team to create a good business story and vision.

Here are a few other responsibilities of a business coach:

- Optimize the alignment of the entire organization
- Increase accountability within teams and individuals in the organization
- Strengthen the company culture
- Increase the focus of the organization
- Make better decisions regarding the 'people.'
- Develop strategies that are more effective in growing the business

A business coach can target individual clients, group clients, or corporate clients. In most cases, business coaches aim to market their services to corporate clients, as that is where they can bill the most hours at the highest rates. However, there are still a plethora of clients that fall into the individual category. Most of the time, these are people who have already started their small to medium-sized businesses and are looking to grow it further by creating a vision, or the clients are people that do not have their own business yet, but their goal is to build their own. The business coach in both these cases help assess what the client's current state is in terms of their business and help them create the vision and plan that is needed to grow their business to a state where they want it to be.

Depending on what type of client the business coach has, they could deliver their sessions in person, over the phone, or by video conferencing. Most corporate companies that hire business coaches likely would require them to come into their workplace to deliver these sessions, whereas entrepreneur type clients may deem over the phone sessions sufficient. Business coaches typically have some sort of background or career within that field. This can range from having run their own business before, or has worked management or executive-level position in the business field and has a good grasp on how businesses work and how to grow it in terms of size, revenue, and vision.

Like I mentioned earlier, there isn't a specific prerequisite for any type of coaching. You must be able to assess yourself and see where your strongest skills lie for you to determine what coaching niche makes the most sense for you. Some business coaches specialize within coaching entrepreneurs only, while others will take clients that are established and entrepreneurs.

5. <u>Performance Coaching</u>

Performance coaches are focused on helping clients that need to improve their performance or abilities for a specific task that they likely have or want a career in. For instance, performance coaches can help a client who is a professional snowboarder and is looking to discover their full potential to reach their goals. Their goals can range from simply winning a competition or qualifying for the winter Olympics. Consequently, performance coaching can also be required for people that aren't athletes. For instance, writers can seek the help of a performance coach in order to get an idea of what their full potential is when it comes to writing. The performance coach can help assess where they are in terms of their writing skill, assess their work, and help guide the client into creating a vision and a set of goals that can be accompanied by an action plan. Performance coaching is one of those coaching types where it's almost necessary to specialize even further. Some performance coaches only coach people in the performing arts like ballet, while other performance coaches may only focus on half-pipe snowboarding.

Performance coaches are responsible for facilitating conversations with their clients so that the clients are encouraged to set goals that are achievable and are working towards a larger goal. These coaches also help their clients build their self-awareness so that they can identify and overcome any challenges and obstacles that they may face when they are looking to improve their desired skill.

Performance coaching is mainly non-directive, which means that the coach does not tell the client exactly what to do or how to do something. However, performance coaching more so focuses on helping the client if they have lost their way or need advice on certain matters. This type of coaching is mainly done via in-person sessions due to the coach needing to assess the client's skill level at a certain activity. It is also crucial that the coach helps the client discover things that they didn't even know that they needed to know. For this, the coach and the client need to have meetings face to face as body language speaks loudly for uncovering growth areas.

If you are someone that is looking to do performance coaching, it is ideal to specialize even further within a skill that you are confident that you have a lot of knowledge on. For instance, if you have been a snowboarder your whole life and you want your side hustle to be performance coaching, then it will be beneficial for you to advertise your coaching business as performance coaching that specializes in snowboarding. Due to your history and experience with this sport, you are able to gain a lot of credibility when you are marketing your services and pitching your ideas to clients.

Performance coaching can be done individually, in groups, or in corporate situations. Most of the time, it is done on an individual basis, but there corporate companies that may seek out this type of service. For instance, dance studios or boot camp companies may seek out a performance coach to help their clients further build upon their skills.

Chapter 10: Money Management 101

With all your new knowledge in financial intelligence, discipline training, goal setting, habit building, mindset development, and side gig/entrepreneur ideas, it is time to learn how to manage the extra money that you'll be saving and making. In this chapter, I will be briefly walking you through what a good money manager looks like and the basics of money management. This will include topics on; basic financial statements and simple investing knowledge.

What Does a Good Money Manager Look Like?

Good money managers always share the same three characteristics. Firstly, they never spend beyond their means, ever. Even if there was a significant opportunity, they will never take out more money than they have to invest in it. Secondly, they always have a good stash of emergency savings. This is where they have money saved up for a rainy day, so they don't have to go into debt or bankruptcy. Thirdly, good money managers assess their risks before taking one. This does not mean they don't take any risks at all because as an entrepreneur, you have to take risks. However, they take calculated risks.

Let's cover the first characteristic first.

- Good Money Managers Will Never Spend Beyond Their Means

Good money managers will never spend more than what they already have. What does this mean? This means that they will never spend more money than they have in their immediate accounts. Most good money managers will have some savings reserved for emergency purposes. That stash of money does not get touched unless it is for emergencies. They also will never take out a loan or pay for things with a credit card if they don't already have that existing money in their debit accounts. Not spending beyond your means will prevent you from getting yourself into debt. Moreover, most people that spend beyond their means usually spend their money on non-essential things. They may be tempted to buy a new car as a big sale at a local dealership is temping them due to low monthly rates. Good money managers will not spend their money on a new car unless it is utterly essential for their living. They need to be 100% sure they can pay off the car without needing to sign up for ridiculously high-interest rates or long financing terms.

- Good Money Managers Always Have Emergency Savings

Emergencies happen to everyone. It can come in the form of a flooded basement or a large medical bill. Good money managers are people that avoid living paycheck to paycheck. Instead, they make an effort to save at least 10% of their income every month into their emergency savings. The purpose of emergency savings is to prevent unforeseen circumstances from bankrupting you. Those who live paycheck to paycheck without any sort of emergency savings can be thrown into financial turmoil if they are suddenly stuck with a $5,000 medical bill. As a rule of thumb, aim to have $10,000 of emergency savings that you can dip into if an expensive accident happens. This will prevent you from needing to stress or needing to take out a high-interest loan to pay for the emergency.

- Good Money Managers Take Calculated Risks

Good money managers only take calculated risks. You often hear of people purchasing and selling stocks to make a lot of money quickly. Although this does work, there is a ton of risk involved. Good money managers usually would not take risks such as purchasing stock as there is no guaranteed return. Instead, they usually use their money to invest in other financial products that have less risk. For instance, a common investment that good money managers like to invest in is real estate. Although you require quite a hefty initial sum of money, the return on it is usually quite high. Here is an example. Kate has savings of $30,000 and is looking for an investment. She is deciding between investing her $30,000 into several different types of stocks or using her $30,000 as a down payment for a house. If Kate were a good money manager, the choice she would make would be to invest $30,000 in a house as long as the real estate in her market is steady. Usually, house prices increase by 5% - 10% every year, which guarantees her an investment return of 5% - 10%. If she chooses to invest her $30,000 into stocks, she is putting her money at a lot of risks as stocks can drop in price in a matter of days while the housing market typically takes longer to drop, and you are provided with much more notice. Simply just by looking at these two options, a good money manager will see that investing in real-estate is the safer choice with high returns. If you are just starting out in managing your money, don't dabble with stocks unless you have knowledge and experience first.

Understanding Basic Financial Statements

In this sub-chapter, I will be teaching you how to read and analyze your basic financial statements. These statements are usually; income statements, balance sheets, and cash flows. If you are someone who has gone to business school or taking finance/accounting at a college or university level, you probably already know this information. If not, you will want to pay extra attention. This will apply to you even more once you start your own business or begin investing your money. Let's start by learning income statements first.

Income Statements

An income statement is a bare minimum that you would need to know in order for you to manage the finances of your business. The purpose of an income statement is simple; it tells you whether you are profiting or losing money. Here is an example of a very simple income statement of a child's allowance:

Revenue or Gross Income: $5.00
Expenses: $2.00 (Candy)
Net Income: $3.00

See how simple this is? The first line is the money that is coming into your possession, while the second line is the money going out of your possession. The bottom line is the difference between the two. Since the number is positive, it means you are making money. If the net income is negative, it means you are losing money. Income statements can be as simple as such, but it does get more complicated the larger your company gets.

As companies grow larger and larger, they include a few more variations of the same structure. For instance, they may have additional lines such as; "cost of revenue" or "gross profit." They may also have additional lines differentiating their income, such as; "operating income" or "income before taxes." Entrepreneurs need to ensure that their income statements are accurate because they need to see whether their business is succeeding or not. An inaccurate income statement can cause you to think that your business is making more than it actually is (bad scenario), or it's making less than you think it is (better scenario).

Balance Sheets

The balance sheet is simple to understand. Its purpose simply is to tell you more about the health of your business. There are three main numbers you should care about in a balance sheet; assets, liabilities, and shareholder's equity. Equity is simply the difference between assets and liabilities. If you have more liabilities than assets, it means that your company is at a deficit. If you have more assets than liabilities, then your company is at a surplus. Let's take a look at assets first. Companies typically have current assets and non-current assets. Current assets are items of value that your business owns that will be converted into cash within one year. A company's current assets include their; accounts receivable, inventory, and cash. The accounts receivable are short-term payments that are owed to your business. The simplest example would be the outstanding invoices that your clients will pay shortly. Inventory is for businesses that sell physical products such as electronics, clothing, furniture, ...etc. Cash can include hard currency, checks, and unrestricted bank accounts. Secondly, you will need to take a look at your non-current assets. These are assets that can't be converted to cash as easily or within one year. This can be both tangible and intangible assets; tangible assets are physical things such as equipment, machinery, or property. Intangible assets are non-physical things such as patents, copyrights, and goodwill. Non-current assets are usually calculated with depreciation factored in which is the cost of the asset over its lifespan. Thirdly, we have our liabilities. Liabilities are a company's financial obligations that are owed to someone else. There are two types of this as well; current liabilities and long-term liabilities. Current liabilities are short-term liabilities that need to be paid within one year; this includes; payments towards long-term debts, payroll, and accounts payable. Long-term liabilities are financial obligations that are due in more than one year's time; this includes; loans and debts. Lastly, there is your shareholder's equity. Shareholders' equity means your business's total net worth. This includes the initial sum of money that the owner invested in the company. If you decide to invest your first year's net earnings into your business, you will report those numbers under shareholders' equity.

Your balance sheets are typically divided into two sides. A balance sheet is correct when both sides are equal to each other. The two sides on a balance sheet are your assets and financial obligations. The main formula of this sheet is Assets = Liabilities + Shareholders Equity.

Here is a simple example of a balance sheet from a printing company.

Assets
- Current Assets:
    - Bank Account: $3470.00
    - Petty Cash: 50.00
    - *Total Current Assets: $3520.00*
- Fixed Assets:
    - Vehicle: $4500.00
    - Printer: 1800.00
    - *Total Fixed Assets: $6300.00*
- Inventory:
    - Stock: $1500.00
- Total Assets: $11,320.00

Liabilities
- Current Liabilities:
    - Accounts Payable: $1800.00
    - *Total Current Liabilities: $1800.00*
- Long Term Liabilities
    - Vehicle Loan: $4500.00
    - *Total Long Term Liabilities: $4500.00*
- Total Liabilities: $6300.00

Equity
- Initial Investment: $5000.00
- Drawings: -$130.00
- Current Earnings: $150.00
- Total Equity: $5020.00

Following the balance sheet equation: Assets = Liabilities + Shareholders Equity, our equation would look like this:

Assets = $6300.00 + $5020.00
$11,320.00 = $11,320.00

Therefore, our balance sheet is correct.

Cash Flows

The cash flow statement is crucial in all businesses as it shows us how the company is spending its money and where their money is coming from. The cash flow statement will show you everything from all the cash it is receiving from its operations and all the cash that is leaving to pay for business costs and investments. A cash flow statement will have three distinct sections; operations, investing, and financing. Here is how a typical cash flow statement will look like:

Cash Flow From Operations

This section of the cash flow statement shows us how much cash is coming from the income statement. A few items under this section are accounts receivables, payables, and income taxes payable. If a client pays their invoice, it will be completed as a receivable transaction, which means it will be recorded under operations. Any changes in a company's current assets or liabilities are also recorded as cash flow from operations.

Cash Flow From Investing

This second record the cash flows that come from sales and purchases of long-term investments (fixed assets) such as equipment and property. Examples of this would be purchases of land, furniture, vehicles, or buildings. Usually, investing transactions will generate cash outflows such as expenditures for equipment, property, plant, business acquisitions, or the purchase of investment securities. Cash inflows will come from the sales of these assets.

Cash Flow From Financing

Debt and equity transactions are reported in this section. Any type of cash flows that include the repurchase/sale of bonds and stocks and payment of dividends are considered cash flows for financing activities. Cash that you receive from a loan or cash that you use to pay off a loan is also recorded in this section.

Here is a sample cash flow:

Harry's Bistro
May 2020

Cash Flows From Operating Activities
- Net Income: $98,285.71
- Receipts From Customers: $76,082.77
- Payments to employees and suppliers: -$32,846.13
- Total adjustments to reconcile net income to net cash provided by operations: $43,236.44
- *Total cash flows from operating activities: $141,522.35*

Cash Flows From Investing Activities
- Computer Equipment: -$1283.49
- Other cash items from investing activities: $2464.84
- *Total cash flows from investing activities: $1181.35*

Cash Flows Financing Activities
- Other cash items from financing activities: $5000.00
- *Total cash flows from financing activities: $5000.00*

Net cash increase for the period: $147,703.70

Cash Balances:
- Net cash increase for the period: $147703.70
- Cash at the beginning of the period: $52,819.91
- Cash at the end of the period: $200,523.61

Simple Investing for Individuals

Now, let's start learning about the basics of investing. Investing is another good way to grow your money and turn it into passive income. However, certain investments can be risky, so learning about the different types is important for you to decide which ones you want to pursue and which ones may require more knowledge and research. Let's take a look.

Stocks

Stocks are one of the most basic forms of investment and likely the most common one you hear about. In the most basic explanation, stocks are securities that represent an ownership share in a company. Companies will issue stocks as a way to raise money from the general public to grow and invest in their own business. Stocks are then exchanged in the stock market. The stock market, such as the New York Stock Exchange, is made up of exchanges. Stocks are listed on a specific exchange and allow sellers and buyers to come together where they can sell/buy shares of certain stocks. The exchange tracks the supply and demand, which usually directly relates to the price or each stock.

Stock prices fluctuate daily, and people who own stocks hope that with time, the stocks that they own will increase in value. For instance, if you bought a stock for company A for $20 apiece, and that stock grows to be worth $50 apiece in three years, you have made $30 over a 3-year period ($10 per year). However, stocks carry some of the highest risks compared to other investments, but it also does have the potential to reap higher rewards. Some people look at stocks as a type of 'gambling' as it is difficult to predict the increase/decrease of stocks. Take a look at bitcoin; for example, what used to be a $7 stock grew to be worth $7000 per stock in the past few years. Although this may sound promising, it can happen the other way around too. You can buy a bitcoin stock for $7000 now and hope that it will grow to $14,000 or more. However, it could drop down back to $7, causing you to lose significant amounts of money.

Bonds

Different from a stock, a bond is a loan taken out by a company, but instead of asking a bank for this money, they ask investors for money by asking them to purchase bonds. In exchange for capital, the company will pay an annual interest rate on the bond, annually or semiannual, and then returns the principal loan on the maturity date. There are six features that you should look out for before purchasing a bond:

- Maturity: This is the date when the bond is paid, and when the initial chunk of money is returned back to you. Maturity is often divided up into; short-term (1 – 3 years), medium-term (10+ years), and long-term (20+ years)

- Secured/unsecured: A bond can either be secured or unsecured. A secured bond promises the bondholders specific assets if the company cannot repay its obligation. This can also be called collateral. If the bond issuer defaults, then the asset is transferred back to the investor. Unsecured bonds are the opposite. They are not backed up by any collateral. These bonds will return only a little bit of your investment if the company fails.

- Liquidation Preference: When a company declares bankruptcy, it will repay its investors in a particular order as they liquidate their assets. Senior debt is debt that will be paid first, and junior debt will be paid last. Stockholders will then get whatever is left.

- Coupon: The coupon amount refers to the interest paid to bondholders either annually or semiannually. The Coupon can be referred to as the nominal yield or the 'coupon rate.' To calculate this, divide your annual payments by the face value of your bond.

- Tax Status: Most corporate bonds are taxable investments, but government/municipal bonds are exempt from tax. Any income or capital gains will be taxed. However, tax-exempt bonds will have a lower interest rate than taxable bonds.

- Callability: Some bonds can be paid off by the company before its maturity. A company may choose to call its bonds if the interest rate allows them to borrow at better rates.

Commodities

Commodities are an important part of an average American's daily life. In its simplest form, a commodity is a basic good that can be used in commerce to interchange with other goods that are in the same category. For example, grains, beef, gold, natural gas, and oil are traditional commodities. For investors, commodities are an important way to diversify portfolios beyond just traditional securities. Since prices of commodities usually move in opposition to stocks, investors rely on commodities during periods of market volatility. Professional traders usually do commodity trading as it is more complicated and does require quite a bit of knowledge and education to pull off effectively. For that reason, I won't go into detail about how commodities are traded and the functions.

REIT

REIT stands for Real Estate Investment Trust. A REIT is a company that operates, owns, or finances income-generating real estate. REITs are modeled after mutual funds and pool capital of numerous investors. This allows investors to earn dividends from various real estate investments without needing to buy, finance, or manage any of these properties themselves. Typical properties in a REIT portfolio include hotels, apartment complexes, healthcare facilities, data centers, or it can also be in the form of telecommunications such as; fiber cables and cell towers. REITs also require a bit more knowledge in the realm of real-estate as some REIT portfolios are a mixed bag of different properties. I don't recommend REITs for beginner investors as there are many risk factors and areas where you must learn about them. However, lots of professional investors and traders swear by REITs, so if this is something you'd like to do, please do some heavy research and learn

about the REITs in your market before investing
any money.

Chapter 11: Basic Financial Terms for Money and Business Management

If you fully understood the previous chapter, then you are well-equipped to dive a little deeper in terms of financial numbers. In this chapter, I will be teaching you about important financial terminology. These are numbers that you absolutely need to know in order to run a successful business and to manage your investments. I will also teach you how to properly understand them and help you analyze what the meaning of these numbers is. You will be learning about ROI, margins, break-evens, and fixed/variable costs. Don't worry; I will also teach you how to calculate each of these numbers. Let's get started.

Return on Investment (ROI)

Whether you are an investor or business owner, return on investment is an important analytical tool that you will need to use. The definition of ROI is the ratio of a profit/loss that is made in a fiscal year expressed in terms of an investment. This number is always expressed as a percentage increase or decrease as it relates to the value of the investment during that fiscal year. Here is a simple example: if you invested $200 in stock and its value rises to $220 at the end of that fiscal year, your return on investment is 10%. In a more complicated example, if you invested $1000 in coffee bean stock for your coffee business and at the end of the year, you generated $2200 from selling coffee made by the beans (assuming no other costs or taxes are involved), your ROI is 220%.

Here is the formula for **ROI**: Net Profit/Total Investment x 100% = **ROI**

Imagine that you are in the business of flipping houses. You purchased a cheap house during a courthouse auction for $75,000 and then spent $35,000 in materials for renovations. After the sales of the house, commission, and expenses, you made $160,000 on the house. What would be your ROI?

First, you have to calculate your net profit, which is your total revenue subtracted with your total costs. In this case, that would be $160,000 − ($75,000 + $35,000), this gives you $50,000. Remember, your costs are the purchase of the house ($75K) and the money you spend on materials ($35K).

Since ROI = Net Profit/Total Investment x 100
ROI = (50,000/110,000) x 100
ROI = 45 x 100
ROI = 45%

This may make house flipping sound easy, but bear in mind that you can also lose money on an investment like this. If your investment is a loss, this formula will give you a negative number. Let's say, after everything; you could only sell the house for $90,000 as there are no other buyers.

Take a look at the new ROI:
Revenue – Total Cost = Net Profit
$90,000 - $110,000 = -$20,000

ROI = Net Profit/Total Investment x 100
ROI = (-20,000/110,000) x 100
ROI = -0.182 x 100
ROI = -18.2%

Essentially, you want your business to be yielding a positive number from your ROI; the higher, the better. If you are yielding a negative number, you may have to start rethinking your business plan or aiming to lower the cost of business.

Margins

In the world of finance, there are various types of margins. The one that is most popularly used is the Profit Margin. There are also Operating Profit Margin, Net Profit Margin, and The Bottom Line. We will learn about all three of these in this chapter. Usually, a company's profit is calculated in three categories on its income statement. The most basic would be their gross profit and the most comprehensive being their net profit. In between these two exists the operating profit.

Gross Profit Margin

Let's start with the gross profit margin first. The gross profit margin is the profit of a business after accounting for the cost of goods sold (COGS). COGS includes the expenses that are DIRECTLY related to production and manufacturing, such as labor wages and raw materials. For instance, if you are a coffee bean seller, your COGS will be the cost of coffee beans purchased. Other figures are excluded in this figure, such as taxes, debt, overhead costs, operating costs, and large expenditures like the purchase of equipment. Here is the formula for the Gross Profit Margin:

Gross profit margin = (Net Sales – COGS)/Net Sales

Here is an example of gross profit margin: Imagine you are a café owner. You have spent $700 on goods such as; coffee beans, milk, and sugar. You also have one employee that you pay approximately $1200 per month. This month, you have $2400 in revenue. What is your gross profit margin?

COGS = $700 + $1200
COGS = $1900

Gross profit margin = (Net Sales − COGS)/Net Sales
Gross profit margin = (2400 = 1900)/2400
Gross profit margin = 500/2400
Gross profit margin = 0.208
Gross profit margin = 20.8%

Operating Profit Margin

Operating profit margin is slightly more complex as it takes into account all other expenses such as; sales expenses, administrative expenses, operating expenses, and overhead expenses. These are all expenses that are necessary to keep the business running on a day-to-day business. This figure, however, still excludes non-operational expenses like debts and taxes. However, it DOES include the depreciation and amortization of assets. Here is the formula for operating profit margin:

Operating profit margin = (operating income/revenue) x 100

Let's use the same example above for this calculation. Here are the other expenses for your coffee shop: Rent is $300 per month, depreciation of your equipment such as coffee machines is $100 per month. Let's calculate your operating profit margin.

Revenue = $2400
COGS = $1900
Rent = $300

Depreciation = $100

Gross Profit = Revenue − COGS
Gross profit = 2400 − 1900
Gross profit = 500

Operating expenses = rent + depreciation
Operating expenses = 300 + 100
Operating expenses = 400

Operating income = Gross profit − Operating expenses
Operating income = 500 − 400
Operating income = 100

Operating profit margin = (operating income/revenue) x 100
Operating profit margin = (100/2400) x 100
Operating profit margin = 0.041 x 100
Operating profit margin = 4.1%

Net Profit Margin

So the net profit margin, otherwise known as the infamous "bottom line." This is the total amount of revenue that is left over after ALL expenses, and income types are accounted for. This will include the operational expenses we just talked about, COGS, and also other expenses such as taxes, debts, and any other payments. This number reflects a business's ability to generate profit from its income. There are two formulas for this number:

Net profit margin = ((Revenue – COGS – Operating Expenses – Other expenses – Interest – Taxes)/Revenue) x 100

Net profit margin = (Net income/Revenue) x 100

Let's carry on with the coffee shop example we've used to calculate the net profit margin. Let's introduce other expenses that this coffee shop has. Imagine that this coffee shop needs to pay $250 in monthly taxes and $20 of monthly interest.

Taxes = $250
Interest = $20

Net profit margin = ((Revenue – COGS – Operating Expenses – Other expenses – Interest – Taxes)/Revenue) x 100

Net profit margin = ((2400 – 1900 – 400 – 20 – 250)/2400) x 100
Net profit margin = (-170/2400) x 100
Net profit margin = -0.07 x 100
Net profit margin = -7%

As you can see through our series of calculations at first glance, using the Gross profit margin, you would think that your coffee shop business is profitable. Even at the operating profit margin level, the business is still profitable. However, when you factor in ALL your expenses by calculating your net profit margin, aka your bottom line, your business is actually not profitable at all. By analyzing all three of these numbers, you are able to get an idea of whether your business is truly profitable or not.

Fixed/Variable Costs

Now, let's learn about fixed and variable costs. The two main costs that a company has are variable costs and fixed costs. The variable cost differs based on the amount that a business is producing. Fixed costs remain the same regardless of how much output the business is producing. Let's take a look at variable cost first.

Variable Cost

A company's variable cost is directly related to the amount of goods/services it is producing. This cost will decrease or increase based on the production volume. When business production increases, the variable cost will rise. If the business product decreases, then the variable cost will decline. Variable costs will differ widely between various industries. This means that it is not useful for you to compare the variable costs of a coffee shop to a car manufacturer because their product output is entirely different. It is much better to compare the variable costs between two companies within the same industry, such as another coffee shop.

Variable costs are calculated by multiplying the quantity of output by the variable cost per unit of output. For instance, let's say company A produces ceramic plates for $2 per plate. If this company produces 500 units, the variable cost will be $1000. However, if the company has no orders and therefore does not produce any plates, then the variable cost would be $0. If the company gets a large order of 10,000 plates, then the cost would rise to $20,000. This calculation does not take into account other costs, such as raw materials or labor.

Fixed Cost

A fixed cost is the other cost that any business or company will have. Different from the variable cost, the fixed cost does not change based on the volume of production. It will remain consistent even if no goods/services are produced. This means that this cost cannot be avoided.

Let's use the same example for company A. Imagine that company A has a fixed cost of $10,000 per month for the rental of their plate producing machine. If the company has no orders for that month and doesn't produce any plates, they still have to pay $10,000 for the machine rental. However, let's imagine that they get a massive order of one million plates; the rental of that machine remains the same; $10,000. However, the variable cost will be $2M in this example.

The higher the fixed cost is for a company, the more revenue they will require to break even. This means that the company will need to sell more products and work harder because these costs usually are unable to be lowered. The most common fixed costs examples are; building leases/rent payments, certain salaries, interest payments, insurance, and utilities.

Variable costs tend to remain consistent based on the number of goods the company produces, but the effects of fixed costs on a company's bottom line can differ based on the number of goods it produces. When production goes up, fixed cost decreases. The price of a larger amount of goods can be spread out over the amount of a fixed cost. Due to this, a company can achieve economies of scale.

For instance, if company A has a $10,000 monthly lease on its factory and it produces 1000 plates per month. It can spread the fixed cost of the lease at $10 per plate. ($10,000/1000 plates) However, if company A produces 10,000 plates per month, then the fixed cost of its lease goes down to $1 per plate.

Break-Even Analysis

The break-even analysis helps a business owner examine their margin of safety for their company based on their collected revenue and all costs. They can use this analysis to analyze different price levels and different demand levels. Essentially, the break-even analysis is used to determine what levels of sales are necessary to 100% cover the company's total fixed costs.

A break-even analysis is useful to determine the required level of production or the targeted desired sales mix. This analysis is normally used by management as these calculations and numbers aren't relevant to external people such as financial institutions, regulators, and investors. This analysis will depend on the calculation of the BEP (break-even point). The BEP is calculated by dividing the total fixed costs of production by the price of a product per individual unit minus the variable cost of production.

The break-even analysis will take a look at the number of fixed costs relative to the profit earned by each unit sold and produced. Usually, a company with lower fixed costs will have a lower BEP. For instance, if your company has $0 of fixed costs, you will break even automatically, and your first sale will generate a profit (considering that variable costs do not exceed your sales revenue).

The break-even analysis involves another financial figure, which is the contribution margin. The contribution margin is the difference between the selling price of a product and the total variable costs. So, let's say you are selling winter jackets for $100 each. The total fixed costs are $25 per unit for the sowing machine lease, and the total variable costs (cost of material) are $60 per jacket. The contribution margin of your jacket is $40 ($100 - $60). The remaining $40 is the amount of revenue that you will need to use to cover your remaining fixed costs, such as your $25 sowing machine lease and other costs like your rent or utilities.

The calculation of a break-even analysis can utilize two equations. The first equation divides the total fixed costs by the unit contribution margin. Let's use the example above of the jacket manufacturer; let's say the total value of fixed costs if $20,000. If they have a contribution margin of $40, the BEP (break-even point) is 500 units (20,000/40 = 500). This means that when you can sell 500 jackets, the payment of your fixed costs is completed, and the company will have a net profit/loss of $0.

You can use a different calculation for the BEP in sales dollars by dividing the total fixed costs by the contribution margin ratio. The contribution margin ratio is calculated by dividing the contribution margin per unit by the sale price. So if we use the same example, the contribution margin is 40% ($40 CM/$100 sale price/jacket = 40%). Therefore, the BEP in sales dollars is $50,000 ($20,000/40% = $50,000).

Chapter 12: Basic Must-Knows for Sales and Expenses

With your new knowledge of crucial financial figures like break-even analysis and fixed/variable costs, I can now teach you strategies to increase sales and reduce expenses. This chapter will be important to you if your primary method to make more money is to start your own business.

How to Increase Sales

There are various different ways a business can try to increase their sales. We will be taking a look at distribution channels, sales mixes, and product selection.

Distribution Channels

The definition of distribution channels is quite simple. A distribution channel is the chain of businesses through which your goods/services will pass before it reaches the end consumer. Wholesalers, distributors, the internet, and retailers are different types of distribution channels. There are two types of questions you need to ask yourself to get an understanding of what your distribution channels are. "Who is my company's suppliers?" and "How do I get my product to the end buyer?"

Think about distribution channels like a map. This is the map of how your goods/services must travel in order for it to reach the end customer. On the other hand, it also describes how the consumer can make payments to get to the original vendor. Distribution channels can be very long or short; it highly depends on how many intermediaries are involved in delivering your service or product. Increasing the number of distribution channels, so it's easier for a consumer to find your goods, is a possible strategy to increase sales. However, having more intermediaries can make distribution management more expensive to manage. Having longer distribution channels could also cause you to earn less profit per item sold.

There are two types of distribution channels; direct and indirect. A direct channel is where the customer is able to buy goods from the manufacturer directly, while an indirect channel allows the customer to buy your goods from a retailer or wholesaler. Indirect channels are the traditional way that goods are sold in your brick and mortar retail store. For example, if you own a coffee shop business and a customer buys coffee beans from you, that is a direct-distribution channel. However, if your customer buys your beans at their local grocery shop and not at your store, that is an indirect channel.

There are three main types of distribution channels, and they are all a combination of producer, wholesaler, retailer, and end customer. The first type of distribution channel is the longest as it includes the producer, wholesaler, retailer, and customer. The best example to describe this channel is the alcohol industry since many laws and regulations are surrounding the selling and purchasing of alcohol. A typical winery is not allowed to sell their products directly to a retailer. Instead, they have to operate on a three-tier system, which means that the winery has to sell their products to a wholesaler first who then will sell the same product to a retailer. Then lastly, the retailer sells the same product to the customer.

The second type of distribution channel removes the wholesaler stage. This is where the producer sells their goods directly to a retailer who then sells the product to the customer. The total amount of intermediaries in this distribution channel is one. A good example of this is Dell. They are a large enough computer company that can sell their goods directly to large retailers such as Best Buy or Walmart.

The third type of distribution channel is the direct-to-consumer model, where the producer sells its products directly to the end customer. An example of this is a typical mom and pop shop like a bakery or a restaurant. They use their own store to sell directly to the end customer. This is the shortest type of distribution channel out there as it cuts out the retailer and the wholesaler.

Sales Mix

The sales mix of a business is a calculation that determines how much of each product/service a business sells relative to the total sales. The sales mix is an important concept to understand and analyze as some services or products that a business offers can be more profitable than others. If a company changes its sales mix, its profits change as well. Managing your sales mix is a strategy and tool that business owners use to maximize company profits.

Many investors will utilize a company's sales mix to determine a company's prospects for profitability and overall growth. If they find that the company's profits are declining or flat, they may stop marketing or even stop selling a certain low-profit product and focus their efforts on selling their high-profit product.

As we learned in the earlier chapter, the profit margin is a company's net income divided by its total sales. This number is used to compare the profitability of two products that may be sold at different prices. Let's use an example. Let's say your coffee shop generates a net income of $15 on a coffee machine that sells for $300 and a net income of $2 on a bag of coffee beans that sells for $10. The profit margin on the bag of coffee beans is 20% ($2/$10 x 100%), and the coffee machine generates a profit margin of 5% ($15/$300 x

100%). This means that selling coffee beans is much more profitable than selling coffee machines, and as the café owner, you may want to shift your marketing efforts to promote your coffee beans as they bring you the highest profit margin.

Product Selection/Differentiation

Product selection or product differentiation is a marketing strategy that aims to distinguish your company's products or services from your competition's products or services. Successfully using product differentiation will require you to identify and communicate the unique qualities of your company's product/service offerings while emphasizing the differences between what you are offering and what other companies are offering. Your company's product differentiation works alongside your company's value proposition to make your products and services as attractive as possible to your audience or target market.

Product differentiations work to give your business a competitive advantage and to build brand awareness. For instance, the fastest high-speed internet (fiber optic) on the market right now is a differentiated product as few internet companies have this service.

The purpose of product differentiation is to convince the customer to choose your brand over a crowded industry of competitors. It is a set of qualities that set your product apart from other similar products. A common strategy that can be used for differentiation marketing is to focus your products and services on a niche market. For instance, a small company may find it hard to compete with larger competitors (e.g., local burger joint versus McDonald's). However, the smaller company may highlight a feature that their competitors don't have, such as better customer service or money-back guarantee.

There are three main types of product differentiation; price, performance, and location. Price is something that can work both ways; you can choose to charge the lowest price possible to attract cost-conscious buyers. You could also charge a higher price to emphasize that your product/service is a luxury service and is worth it, such as a luxury car. Performance and reliability is another type of product differentiation. Traditionally, products that are considered reliable and could last a long-time is seen as better than other competitors.

An example of this is a washing machine that is advertised to last for 20+ years may generate more sales than a washing machine that is advertised to last 5+ years only. Lastly, location can be a huge product differentiation, especially for smaller companies. These smaller companies usually market their brand as a local business and emphasize their more personal service as a way for them to show customers that their business is worth the higher price.

How to Reduce Expenses

Now, let's take a look at a few strategies and tips that your company can use to reduce its expenses. There are only two ways that you could increase profits for your business; you could either increase your sales or reduce your expenses. Increasing sales is typically the harder route as it will involve a lot of strategies, planning, and moving pieces to pull off. However, reducing business expenses is something that is much easier to do and takes less time. Let's take a look at a few different ways that you can reduce business expenses to generate a larger bottom line.

1. Go digital

Printing costs are a huge expense that most companies don't realize can add up very quickly. The cost of ink, paper, and machine maintenance costs a small fortune, and a lot of time is wasted dealing with silly printing issues. As an entrepreneur, try to eliminate paper usage as much as possible to cut costs and streamline your business. Go digital as much as possible and take advantage of free software like Google drive and online signature services. This will also prevent problems like misplaced documents. Having everything digital will allow you and all of your employees to access important information quickly and cheaply.

2. Buy from big service providers

Big service providers typically have the cheapest prices for materials you require as they can operate on a lower profit margin. Smaller local options may seem better at first glance as they can customize their offerings to meet your needs. However, do some research on the big service providers first to see if they have any customizable offerings. This can help reduce your operating costs significantly.

3. Insurance

Depending on what your company offers, you may need to invest in some insurance. This could be liability insurance, building insurance, or car insurance. You need to regularly review your agreement with your insurance provider to figure out if another company can offer you a better deal. It doesn't take much time to do this, and it can easily save you thousands of dollars every single year while your company is still receiving the same benefits. Some start-up insurance companies offer cheaper insurance premiums as they have lower costs by taking away office spaces and offering fully-remote work to their employees.

4. ## Hiring freelancers instead of staff when possible

Assess your company's needs when you feel like you require new talent to fix a business problem or to improve your business. If you require a website makeover, you don't need to hire a fulltime web developer to do this job. You can hire a freelancer easily to do the same job but without the long-term commitment. Outsource your work to contractors or freelancers whenever you can, but don't cheap out on them. Good contractors and freelancers typically cost a little bit more, but it's much better to pay more upfront for high-quality work then to have to pay someone else to fix it later.

5. ## New equipment does not perform that much better than used equipment

It is nice to buy new items but ensure that you are assessing the value of the new item you are buying in comparison to a similar secondhand item. For instance, if you are starting up your own coffee shop, look around your neighborhood buy and sell websites and forums to see if you can find the espresso machine model that you want but second hand. Most of the time, good equipment remains in good health even after many years, so buying a new espresso machine may not give you any additional benefits. Buying a second-hand machine may cost much less and provide you with the same services that you require.

6. <u>Don't spend money on needless office space</u>

If you are a business that does not regularly have clients coming and going, move your office space to somewhere less expensive or get rid of it altogether. With our convenient technology nowadays, you can even offer remote work for your employees to reduce the amount of physical space you need. If you require weekly meetings with your employees, rent a one-time space, or make it fun by having it at a local restaurant or bar.

Chapter 13: Basic Accounting and Financial Management Tips

All money managers or business owners are faced with risks; a lot of these risks are actually due to improper financial management and decision making. The decisions that you make for yourself and/or business can literally make or break it. When starting a business or an investment, it involves you to consider many things; this includes; what services/goods you are offering, your target market, resources required, and the investment you'd like to make. The question here is, how can you make better choices in all these aspects? Below are some pointers to help you avoid making bad financial decisions.

Tips to Help You Avoid Making Bad Financial Decisions

- Do research

The BEST thing you can do to avoid making bad financial decisions is to do your research. There is nothing that you can achieve without conducting the right research. Whether this is research for your target market or a specific product, it matters just as much. The bigger the decision you need to make, the more research is necessary. Make sure you are researching the potential risks of a business decision before jumping on it. While some risks are worth taking, other risks are not. Take notes and analyze the data that you've found to make the best decision for yourself.

- Prioritize

In business, there are always three major aspects involved. The first aspect is your initial idea for your business. The second aspect is your investment. This is extremely important as your business is limited to how much funds are available to start it. The last investment is time. By optimizing all three aspects, you can ensure that your business is productive.

- Choose the right investment

Not every investment that you make will produce large results. This is because not every investment is the right one. Sometimes, entrepreneurs make bad investments in areas that their company does not benefit from. You need to be asking yourself whether or not your next investment is going to provide you with substantial results. If not, you shouldn't spend that money.

- Don't shy away from making hard decisions

Although this may sound like common sense, the root of bad business decisions is usually due to a person's inability to make tough decisions. Often times as business owners and entrepreneurs, we are faced with hard choices that require an immediate decision. Running a business means that you need to be firm with your decisions. This could range from firing someone who is dragging down your business or breaking free from a partnership. This could even mean giving up on a particular service/product and rethink your business plan entirely.

- Do not delay debt payments

Debt and loans are common aspects of all businesses. There isn't any harm in taking out a loan to invest in your business, but the problem begins if you are unable to repay your debts on time. The more you delay paying off debt, the worse it gets. The interest that will be charged due to late payments is one of the biggest enemies for a business. This can decrease the credit score of your business and financial status. Ensure that when you are taking out a loan, you are sure that you will be able to repay every payment on time. If you are unsure about this, it may not be the right decision for your business at the time. Don't take out any loans if you aren't confident that you will be able to pay it back without delay.

Choosing the Right Accounting Method To Meet Your Needs

Believe it or not, most people don't give their accounting much thought for their small businesses. You may have an accountant that just does your taxes for you without even asking you if you have any preferences. There are two main accounting methods for small businesses; cash vs. accrual basis accounting.

As a money manager, you need to know the difference between these two types of accounting and understand which you are eligible to use and when each method is the best choice for you. With small business taxes, cash basis, or accrual basis accounting can have huge consequences on you. Keep in mind that different countries have different tax regulations, so please consult your accountant on these differences. For example purposes, we will be using U.S. regulations for our examples.

Typically, the IRS will require all businesses to use a consistent and standardized accounting method each year for business taxing. If you decide to use a different accounting method down the line, you have to get approval from the IRS. Let's learn about the functions of cash and accrual methods.

Cash Basis Accounting

A cash basis is the most common method that small businesses use for their accounting. In cash basis accounting, the income that you make is recorded when it's received. For instance, let's say you own a consulting company, and you did work for a client on May 20th. You then created an invoice with a due date of June 1st. You will record the income for your work when the customer pays you in June instead of May when you actually delivered the work. The premise of cash basis accounting is that your income is recorded when you receive your payment from the customer, not when you have delivered the work or billed the customer.

Similarly, your expenses are recorded when you have paid them, not when you have ordered them. Let's say you forgot to pay your office rent in June. When you receive your rent bill in July, you notice that you are billed twice the amount. After you verify that you did indeed not pay the rent for June, you will need to write a check to pay both months' rent by July 1st. You will then record this full payment amount as an expense in July, which means that no rent payment will be recorded in your financial statements for the month of June.

There are many benefits to cash-based accounting, the main one being that record keeping is easy. If you are recording your income as you receive it and expenses as you pay them, you can literally do all your accounting work without needing to hire an external accountant. If you use this method, you don't need to enter bills and invoices into any business/accounting software. However, these functions are still useful as you can then ensure that no expenses or income are being missed. Another benefit to cash basis accounting is that it helps you track your cash flow. Having this analysis handy will allow you to get a good idea of what your business' cash flow is like and how it's changing.

However, there are some downsides to this accounting method. A cash basis can easily give you an unrealistic picture of how your business is doing. Let's look back at the example where you billed your customer in May, but your customer actually paid their invoice in June. Let's say that you did a ton of work at the end of May, but none of your customers paid until June. When you look back on these statements in the future, you may think that May was a very busy month, and June was slow because of the amount of money you received in June. From this information, you may decide to make business decisions such as reducing labor costs in May or even taking some time off then. This can be a huge mistake for your business as the truth is that you were busy in May, not in June. You had simply just received payment for your work in May, in June. Some other downsides to cash basis accounting include difficulty tracking profitability monthly and the need to track accounts payable and receivable separately. Profitability is hard to track per month as sometimes your invoices and expenses aren't paid in the same month, although they were meant for that same month. Let's think back to that example where you forgot to pay rent in June and had to pay double rent in July. Since a double rent payment was paid for in July, it can skew your expenses dramatically and make June look like a more profitable month than July when in reality, the business could've been the same or slightly worse in June.

Accrual Basis Accounting

Larger companies more commonly use accrual basis accounting but smaller ones can benefit from it too. In accrual basis accounting, your business income is recorded when it's earned (opposite from cash basis). Back to the example we used, the work that you've done in May would show up on May's financial statement and not June's. Similarly, expenses are also recorded when it's incurred, not when you pay it. In our missed rent payment scenario, although you forgot to pay June's rent and had to pay it in July, your financial statements would show a rent expense in June.

There are many benefits to accrual basis accounting. The first benefit is that it tracks your business performance much better than cash basis accounting. Accrual basis accounting allows you to easily see when your business is most or least profitable on a monthly basis. Based on your financial statements, you may be able to make accurate business decisions like increasing your workforce during May to accommodate more customers rather than cutting your labor down. Accrual basis accounting helps business owners forecast and budget better. Secondly, accrual basis accounting gives the business owner better abilities to track monthly profits. You can see your true net profit for each month, which helps to prevent the common mistake of overcommitting on expenses. Lastly, accrual basis accounting is typically what investors and lenders prefer. These people want to have a clear view of how your company's doing, and accrual basis accounting is the best way to see this picture clearly.

There are some downsides to this accounting method. Firstly, it makes it harder to detect any cash flow issues. In accrual basis accounting, there is a third financial statement that is critical to your business decisions. Let's go back to that example where you delivered work in May but got paid in June. Your net profit in May is going to look great. However, your bank account may be sitting at $0 because you haven't actually been paid yet. This means that you will want to analyze your profit and loss statements side by side with your cash flow statement to ensure you are being paid. Secondly, this accounting method requires more time and labor to administer. When you are running your financial reports, you have to make sure all your bills for expenses and invoices to the customer have been inputted into your system before you can produce reports. This may make the end of the month stressful, especially if you aren't inputting this information as you go. Hiring a professional accountant in this scenario would be immensely helpful. Lastly, accrual basis accounting can lead to you paying higher taxes. This is because you are recording your income exactly on the date that you earned it, which means that you could be paying taxes on income that haven't actually reached your bank account yet.

Which Accounting Method Is Best for You?

For simplicity's sake, most small business owners will choose cash basis accounting. However, we can't deny the benefits that come with accrual basis accounting if you want to get a realistic read on how your business is doing.

Cash basis accounting is the best method for the following situations:

1. <u>You are just starting your business, and you are a sole proprietor</u>

Cash basis accounting doesn't require as much learning, and studying as accrual-basis accounting does. This is the best method for those that are low on cash and just started their business that is likely juggling many responsibilities at one time. If you can't afford an accountant or don't need it yet, this method is the simplest way to keep track of your finances.

2. <u>You are a business with low investment, and you're preparing for tax season</u>

If your business is new with not that much income coming in yet and you are worried about paying your taxes, cash basis accounting is useful for you as it shows you exactly how much cash you have on hand. For instance, if you had serviced a client before the tax filing deadline, but your client hasn't paid their invoice yet, then you can report that sale for next year's taxes.

Accrual accounting is the best method for the following situations:

1. <u>Your business has an average gross revenue of $25M+ across a three-year period</u>

The IRS is flexible regarding which accounting method you want to use, but if your business averages over $25M, then you have to file your taxes via accrual basis. Any less than that, then you are able to choose whichever accounting method you like.

2. <u>Your business has inventory</u>

Businesses that have inventory were required to utilize accrual basis accounting according to previous law. However, due to recent tax changes, as long as your business has under $25M of revenue in the last three years, you can treat your inventory as non-incidental materials or choose an accounting method that is best for your business.

3. <u>You have to file sales tax</u>

Certain states (like New York) require business owners to file sales taxes on an accrual basis. Be sure to do research in the state that you reside, or else you may find yourself needing to pay sales tax on an invoice that you haven't had payment for yet. This could have terrible effects on your cash flow. In this situation, an accountant would be in your best interest to help you figure out whether or not this applies to your business.

Chapter 14: Basic Legal Must-Knows Before Starting Your Own Business

There are a few legal must-knows you must consider before starting your own business. Although this part of starting up your business may seem boring, it is extremely crucial as not doing some of these steps can lead to legal trouble down the road. We all know how time-consuming and expensive that is, so let's avoid this by being prepared. Here are a few items you need to prepare for, depending on where you are running your business.

1. ### Is your business name legal?

Before you start building your business website, and begin its marketing, make sure that another business doesn't already purchase the name you have chosen. Depending on what country you live in, there should be a free online search where you can look up all business names that are registered. It will then tell you whether or not your business name has already been taken in your residence area. Make sure to do this step before you invest any money into the business name you've come up with.

2. ### Register a DBA or Fictitious Business Name

If your business is running on a different name from your own (e.g., Your name is John Smith, and your business name is 'Wellness Coaching For All'), then you have to register for a DBA (doing business as) to use for filing for all paperwork purposes. This is normal practice for businesses in the U.S. but may vary from country to country. Make sure you look into what your country requirements are and have it completed to avoid any penalties from your government.

3. Incorporate Your Business & Get A Tax ID

We talked about incorporating your business in the previous chapters depending on which country you are from. This is important for all tax purposes, and different business structures have different ways of filing/doing taxes. If you don't do this, you are likely to operate your business illegally and could be faced with numerous fines. Once you decide which business structure you want to go with for your coaching business, you need to register for a tax ID number. This number will function as your business's identification with the government. This will allow the government to audit/track your business transactions. Failure to do this may lead to fines and jail time for evading taxes.

4. Educate Yourself On Employee Laws

Depending on whether you want to grow your business into a firm (where you will hire employees) or not, you must educate yourself on employment laws. If you hire someone to work for your business, you must understand your obligations for taxes, payroll, unemployment insurance, wage & hour requirements, workers' compensation, and anti-discrimination laws. Moreover, you can also hire contractors to avoid some of these liabilities, but you would need to educate yourself on those laws as well. Make sure you get a good understanding before bringing someone else on board to avoid any lawsuits.

5. Obtain the Necessary Business Permits and Licenses

Depending on where you live in the world, your business may require you to get a permit or a license before it can legally operate. Specific to the coaching/consulting businesses we talked about earlier, there are many different types of coaching licenses – make sure you educate yourself on which one you need depending on what your specialization is and your country of residence. You should also look into whether or not you need a special permit to run your coaching business. Most countries do not require this, but it's better to be safe than to have your business shut down for illegal practices.

6. File For Trademark Protection

Although you are not legally required to trademark your business, you can avoid future headaches by trademarking your business name to avoid anybody using your brand for their own benefit. This may not be necessary if you are just starting out your coaching business, but as it becomes more successful and well-known, this is a step that you should remember to do to protect yourself and your business.

7. Open A Business Bank Account

Opening a business bank account for your business will not only help you separate your personal finances from your business ones, but it will also help you build business credit so you can take out loans in the future as needed. Go to your local bank and find the best business banking account deal and make use of their offerings. They usually can offer a business banking account with deals or business credit cards that help you collect points.

Chapter 15: Prioritization Tips for Your Side Hustle

In this final chapter, let's take a look at a few more tips to help you better prioritize your side hustle or business income. These are a few rules that, if you stick to, you will always be moving in the right direction. When in doubt, refer back to these tips to make sure you are prioritizing correctly.

1.   Always Prioritize Your Full-Time Job First

When starting your coaching business or any other side hustle/business, it can be fun, exciting, and very tempting to think about. However, do not allow yourself to be distracted with your business during the working hours of your main job. As side businesses are not steady when they first begin, you should not compromise your main source of income for an unstable source of income. When your business begins to take off and is beginning to bring in equal or more income than your main job, you can consider making it your primary active source of income instead. Until then, make sure you are not compromising your full-time job.

2.   Never take on business debt for your coaching business.

Many businesses require the owner to spend money before they are able to make money. This is why a lot of small/side businesses can take a while before they make a profit. Statistically, many startups end up failing because of their inability to never make a profit. To avoid this, start your business if you can fund it through your savings alone. Or even better, businesses like a coaching business can have a low start-up cost, simply try to avoid any start-up costs in general. Yes, you may have to pay someone to build your website or pay a monthly fee for an online meeting platform, but by minimizing your costs, you can avoid being in debt if you decide to end your business venture.

3. Don't spend money where your customer can't see.

An important tip for all business owners is to spend your money where the customer can see. If your business is growing and you want to invest money into it, rather than buying a new business phone to call your clients, you could invest in creating a meeting space of your own to host your sessions. The more investing you do to the parts of your business that your customers can see, the more difference it makes for them. Without customers, your side business will fail.

4. Spend your money on actual efficiency.

When owning your own coaching business or any business in general, it may be tempting to spend your money on purchasing supplies or buying a certain tool that makes you think you could help you perform faster. However, if you don't have enough clients or customers, then you really don't need to spend money on increasing efficiency. Avoid spending any money to 'improve efficiency' until you feel as if you are actually inefficient. That is when efficiency truly matters.

5. <u>Always schedule specific hours for your coaching business.</u>

We talked about this earlier in the book; scheduling hours specifically for you to work on your business is crucial. When your regular workday ends, your business working hours are starting. Schedule off blocks of time during those hours and stick to it. This will prevent you from giving up quickly because you're 'not seeing progress' if you are consistently putting in the work to start your business.

6. <u>Only do actions that generate revenue.</u>

Although your business will require you to spend time working on the administrative tasks and streamlining the infrastructure, you should not spend all your time there. What you need to focus on is generating business by either selling or working. Spend most of your working hours for your coaching business on marketing and selling your products and services and actually delivering them. All successful entrepreneurs spend more time working FOR their business rather than IN their business.

<u>Conclusion</u>

By the end of this book, the main takeaway is that a good money manager requires you to have the right mindset, discipline, and habits combined with having the financial skills. Having just one or the other may not be enough to help you successfully save money.

When in doubt, always yourself, what does a good money manager look like? There isn't always one answer, but typically, a person that is good at money management are; financially intelligent, resourceful, and frugal. You learned about financial intelligence earlier in this book – this is the foundation of a good money manager. When you are intelligent with your finances and have a knack for knowing what to do with money and how to save more of it, things like investments and entrepreneurship should come naturally to you. To ensure that you are practicing all the main traits of a good money manager, start building upon your financial intelligence, as we discussed earlier on in this book. Then, be resourceful in the ways of bringing in secondary sources of income. Explore side gigs, business ideas, and investments to help you generate more income. Finally, be frugal. Find as many areas as you can in your life right now where you can save money. I taught you a few tips earlier on in this book that can easily save you a few hundred dollars per month. Start implementing those to put yourself in the best spot possible to grow that money further.

Remember always to give back when you find financial success. Help out friends with their new businesses or family members that are struggling. I promise you that this will come back to benefit you someday. Also, this book has provided you with endless tips and strategies. Finding the best strategies that work for you specifically is important. Some people may find that doing side gigs is a great way for them to make more money, whereas another person may have zero success with that. Figuring out what works for you is a part of the process. I wish you the best of luck on your journey. Remember, it's not always about your knowledge of money, but it is also about your attitude and discipline towards it.

Description

Are you someone that's struggling to save money at the end of the month? Are you finding that every dollar of your income is always accounted for? Are you sick of living paycheck to paycheck? If you relate to any of these questions, then you likely need to work on your attitude and beliefs with money, and your actual money management skills. You don't have to feel alone. Most people in North America have struggled with credit card debt, overdue bills, foreclosed homes, and many other negative financial events. Improving your financial intelligence, paired with changing your attitude and beliefs towards money, can help you begin making the changes you need in your life. Learning more about money management and how to read financial statements will help you better understand and control your money if you were to invest it or to grow it. A lot of people become stuck in the misunderstanding that they simply don't have the time or knowledge to make more money or to grow their existing savings. This is simply not true. Many simple and straightforward strategies can allow someone to grow their money or to add an extra income stream. This book will help you with the following:

- What is financial intelligence and how to improve yours

- How to adopt a positive mindset with money and drop any negative beliefs
- Improving your self-discipline with money to save more and spend less
- How to be productive with your savings
- Various money-saving tips and strategies to help you grow your savings account
- How to build healthy money habits to save your money better
- How to get rid of any negative beliefs and thoughts you have with money using various strategies
- The importance of goal setting – how do I set effective money goals?
- Side gig ideas to help you increase your secondary income
- Entrepreneur ideas to help you start your own business and to grow your money
  - Low overhead business ideas with high revenue streams
- The basics of financial statements – how to read and understand them
- The basics of business money management – how to analyze your own business
- The basics of sales and expenses – how you can increase sales and reduce expenses
- Basic accounting and financial management tips
- More tips to avoid making bad financial decisions!

- Basic legal must-knows before investing/starting your own business
- How to prioritize different income streams

Together, the various topics in this book will help you build new thoughts and beliefs related to money so you can change your behavior once and for all. By doing this, you are allowing yourself to be open-minded to different money-savings and income-generating ideas so you can continue to grow your money as much as possible. Everyone can learn to be better with their money; they just have to let go of their own restricting beliefs. Start making effective changes in your life today; money really does matter. Buy *Frugal Living and Money Management* and begin to save more money, make more money, and to grow more money.

www.ingramcontent.com/pod-product-compliance
Lightning Source LLC
Chambersburg PA
CBHW071555210326
41597CB00019B/3252